*"...the India leaf, comfort of
the pensive, delight of
the daydreamer, fragrant bosom
of the winged opal".*

José Martí

To José Antonio Portuondo

Printed and Published in the U.S.A. by
T.F.H. Publications, Inc.
1 T.F.H. Plaza
Neptune City, NJ 07753
U.S.A.

THE JOURNEY OF THE
HAVANA CIGAR

by
Antonio Núñez Jiménez

photography by
Gianni Costantino

T.F.H. PUBLICATIONS, INC.

Prologue

A judicious friend, also a literary observer, told me some time ago that the use of prologues seemed to be returning after several years of absence or obsolescence. This disappearance and return might require some explanation, but in this case we need not go beyond doubts and queries.

What is a prologue: a simple foreword to the main text? a defense of the work and the author before anyone has the chance to contradict them? or perhaps a sibylline manner of allowing the prologist to express his ideas on the subject? Would an epilogue be better, so the author can lay the groundwork for what the closing words say? Let's hold our peace, respecting the academic preferences of the past and seek our way.

Sure, these questions are a concern, i.e. they preface the prologue, when the work in question, like this one, embraces with an informative spirit an entire world, one of those universes created by man in his relentless accumulation of experience down through the centuries. I am referring to the infinite social and scientific implications of tobacco. And what can one say of an author known for the abundance of his previous work? In giving us this book, Antonio Núñez Jiménez, brotherly friend, companion in many shared tasks, has impressed on the tobacco world as a whole his all-encompassing enthusiasm, his encyclopaedic vocation and wealth.

As a well-known geographer and speleologist, he is one of those for whom configurations, structures and natural facts take on meaning only when man delves into them. In this way they can be examined in their most unusual or unexpected associations, their most remote, meaningful implications. In this way nature is transformed into a sort of continuum expressed in and by the history of man, who can learn of periods whem he was not present by contemplating it, suffering it, using it. Thus a specialization becomes an intriguing interest through blending of the two great divisions of science, natural and social.

Were the pages of this book not sufficient to validate this scientific embrace — but they are, of course — we could refer back to the concept of nature culture *characterized by the author in other texts of his creation as a sentiment and conscience which unite beauty and utility without gaps or interposed abuses and with full respect for the authentic social needs of both. Núñez Jiménez seems to avoid pure and simple* ecologism *with great skill, since he does not use the defense of one (nature) to save the other (man) — an absolute necessity in times of provocatory reactionary tempests — but rather builds a safeguard for both, blending them in the interests of progress. In truth, the secret of all the author's achievement lies in his undying use of brevity and updating to project the future. That's it: the point of arrival and departure.*

An implicit step in this contribution by the author is the extension of this concept of culture to the world of tobacco, characterized by an inherent mobility, ever since — how many centuries ago! — some natives of America domesticated the plant, expropriating it from nature. Neither they nor those who came in succesive waves penetrated into the mystery of tobacco's ritualism, nor into the nature of the operations necessary to prepare it for its intended use. Nevertheless, it is quite possible that they discovered which soils were suitable for growing it. Each period added on or forgot something, small or large, about the world of tobacco, its production, commerce, consumption, its social and political implications, its rituals of courtesy, social coexistence or fashion, its scientific repercussions, its motivating presence in the arts. Furthermore, important studies were made reflecting the dynamic nature of the topic, though the encyclopaedic analysis of the subject is a thing of this century, for reasons of diversification and scientific qualities which we shall not seek to explain in these few introductory pages. The reason is that, in each period, the capturing of this ever-combative world was always projected and placed, intelligible and measured, in the hands of those who could not encompass it by themselves.

Nevertheless, scientific concern has been unable to unravel the genealogy of this charming Solanacea. No wild species has been found; all the existing species are hybrids, and many of them are assumed to be the result of pollination by means of diffusive agents, with no special participation by the Amerinds. The Europeans learned of it in 1492, and since then it has constituted a growing branch of agricultural and industrial production of capitalism. A whole history lesson in this regard tells us how European civiliation assimilated into its unbridled pecuniarism the practices of the "savages" it discriminated against and anihilated. This history is characterized by the development of ways to consume it that constitute per se a democratisation process of the smoking habit.

The product processed for the smoker spread through the world, starting with the form used by the Indians (leaves rolled and wrapped in maize or tobacco leaves; in pipes, tubes or other instruments), to the powdered form or snuff, *symbol of courtly prestige, which required the use of mills or grinders, to the* cigarette *prepared by workers in their homes, later in large factories and, finally by machine (19th century), while the* twisted tobacco or *cigar, which like snuff before it, retained an aura of upper social class. There is in all this a pathway destined to spread and generalise the use of tobacco under favorable conditions of presentation, distribution and price. Would it be rash to say that it was the first product to foreshadow excessive materialism by contagion and induction and with no transcendent objective of more recent periods of capitalism?*

Down through the centuries, this world of tobacco suffered the natural aggressions of each period. In the 16th and 17th centuries, it was a therapeutic drug appreciated by medical science in the quest of sedatives and healing products for the plethora of ills and diseases that were difficult to indentify, much less treat and alleviate. Some thought it a panacea, which others denied, and today, all at once, we are synthesizing nicotinic acid for medicinal purposes and debating on the negative effects of tobacco intoxication.

Let us not forget other centuries-long, more challenging battles, often tragic, concerning the aromatic leaf. Battles of the state against smugglers or against competitors in foreign markets and at home; religious and repressive condemnations of tobacco against rebellious consumers; the protests of smokers and growers against the monopolistic excesses of the monarchies pressed for resources; strikes by workers to obtain better working conditions; constant judicial and diplomatic claims against the illegal or ambiguous use of the appelation "Havana cigar", which belonged to Cuba, because of the quality of its leaf; admonitions, warnings and sanctions against smokers in areas of catastrophic danger. Never has the world of tobacco been free of strife, within and without.

Hence the richness of this history, the strenuous work of erudition surrounding it, the role of enthnohistory, social anthropology and literature in its study; the expansion, in other words, of this world, a segment no less important than the culture of Cuban nature, which we receive from Antonio Núñez Jiménez with so much love and wisdom.

Julio Le Riverend

Havana, 10 January 1988

The journey begins

I was smoking with infinite pleasure, seated on the solid base of a stalagmite which rose throne-like in the mouth of an open cave at the foot of the Sierra de los Organos. These tall, steep hills seemed to close off the wide Luis Lazo Valley, while the bright, warm sunlight filtered through the broad, pale-green leaves of a plantain. A light breeze blew from the back of the cave, agitating the spirals of smoke streaming from my Havana cigar, rising, expanding to become castles, hazy images, spreading hair, spiraling waterspouts, highlighted by the slanting angle of the setting sun. Now they headed toward the tobacco plantation that carpeted the entire valley, and I imagined the smoke was returning to its roots. In the distance, the tobacco-planters cultivated the plants that would fill the dreams of smokers the world over.

This is how the idea came to me to write a book recounting the journey of the Havana cigar, from seed to smoke, as seated on my creation rock I reflected that the enjoyment of a cigar requires a lengthy journey, composed of a hundred and forty different operations, a journey not of one day but a matter of years, through the labour of delicate, expert hands, expressing their mastery of the tobacco skills handed down from generation to generation.

Now we invite the reader to accompany us on this exciting journey that takes tobacco from plantation seedbeds to entrancing smoke. We shall stroll together through the world of mythology, science, history and poetry, finally reaching the boundless cosmos, where the Havana cigar has been carried on the wings of spacecraft.

1. *Dawn in the tobacco country of Vuelta Abajo.*

2. *Sprouting of the tobacco plant from seed.*

Mutual discovery

At dawn on 12 October 1492, Indians in the hamlet of Bariay, on the northeastern coast of Cuba, were startled by an amazing sight: three enormous canoes with white sails unfurled, revealing the Christian cross. Hidden among the branches of the wild vines, from a beach of glistening sand, they observed those strange men disembarking. One stood out from the group with his rubicund face and well-proportioned body and the magnificent silk suit he wore. In his right hand he held a red and yellow flag, symbol of the sovereignty of Castille over the lands of the New World.

The aborigenes, torn between curiosity and fear, went forth to meet those beings they assumed had descended from the heavens. Spaniards and Indians examined each other with equal amazement.

Admiral Christopher Columbus christened the place San Salvador; he admired the beauty of the island and the candor of its inhabitants. In his logbook, he wrote: "This is the most beautiful island eyes have ever beheld".

Some days later, Columbus continued sailing westward, and on 29 October disembarked on nearby Bahía de Gibara, at what he called Puerto de Mares.

He was seeking the eastern lands of the Great Khan, attracted by the golden cities described in books on Cathay. And since he thought that kingdom lay in the Cuban interior, on 2 November he sent two of his men, Luis de Torres and Rodrigo de Xerez, to scout for it. The former knew the languages of the Hebrews and the Arabs, in addition to Spanish.

Four days later, the Admiral's envoys returned and described the beauty of the lands they had visited and the paradisiacal customs of the natives, who, far from living in palaces with gold roofs, dwelt in truly rustic huts of palm fronds. But let's hear the report Luis and Rodrigo made to the Genoese mariner, written down later by Fray Bartolomé de las Casas, venerable protector of the American aborigenes:

On their way, these two Christians came across many people walking through the towns, women and men; all the men had firebrands in their hands and certain herbs to breathe in the smoke, dried herbs enclosed in a certain leaf, also dried, a sort of musket made of paper, like those children make on the feast of the Holy Spirit, lit on one end, while on the other they were drawing or sucking, breathing in that smoke; with which they numb their flesh and which is almost intoxicating, and in this way they say they never feel fatigue. These muskets, we shall call them, they call tabaccos. *I met Spaniards in this island Espanola that had the habit of partaking, who when reprimanded for this, saying it was a vice, answered that they were unable to stop partaking; I know not what enjoyment or benefit they derive from it.*

A similar report was made by historian Gonzalo Fernández de Oviedo:

And as they began to drink, the chief himself took up a handful of tobaccos which were a hand-span long and thin as a finger, and were of a certain leaf rolled and tied with two or three fine sisal threads; they grow this leaf and plant with great diligence to obtain these tobaccos, and lighting them at the end, they burn slowly... until they stop burning, which takes a day. From time to time they put the end opposite the burning end in their mouths and draw in that smoke for a brief time and hold it with mouth closed and hold their breath awhile, and then they breathe out and that smoke comes out of their mouths and nostrils. And each of the Indians, I say, held one of these rolled leaves...

As we have seen, Admiral Columbus mentions tobacco and smoking for the first time on Cuban territory; nevertheless, in his diary under 15 October 1492, while near the Island of San Salvador, he refers to a powder and some leaves that could well have been this product:

3. *Preparation for sowing seed in the fields.*

4. *Sowing seed.*

5. *Covering the fields with straw.*

Down the paths of mythology and magic

...And in the gulf between the two islands... I spied a man in a canoe who was crossing from the island of Santa Maria to Fernandina, and he was carrying a little of their bread, about a fistful, and a gourdful of water and a lump of reddish earth powdered and then kneaded, and some dry leaves which must have been very valued, because they had brought me some as a gift on San Salvador...

Don Salvador de Madaraga, in his book *Life of the Most Magnificent Sir Christopher Columbus,* says something so appropriate about the discovery of tobacco by the Europeans that if someday we build a monument to Luis de Torres and Rodrigo de Xerez, the first Spaniards to explore the interior of Cuba, we must carve the words of this Spanish historian on it: "They failed to find the Great Khan or the fountain where gold was born, but they found something which has since kindled more dreams than gold and exercised more power over men than the Great Khan ever exercised over his subjects".

Since the Admiral gave no great importance to the discovery of tobacco, Madariaga comments: "As we are blind to the favors of fortune (...) when Nature placed gold before him in this new, unexpected form, Columbus did not recognize it and let it go up in smoke before his very eyes without appreciating its aroma".

After its discovery by the Spanish, the fragrant leaf won over the taste of the first mariners who, intoxicated in its spiralling smoke, dreamed like new witches or sorcerers of El Dorado and the Fountain of Youth.

These navigators, and later the *conquistadores* and colonists, were unknowingly forging the beginning of a constellation of new states in an almost virgin America.

There are some doubts about what the Indians called tobacco.

Some authors advance the theory that this term was used to designate the Y-shaped instrument they used to inhale the smoke or the tobacco powder, while *cohiba* was the name of the plant. On the other hand, friar Ramón Pané said that "*cojoba* is a powder that they use to purge themselves and other things; they take it with a pipe half-an-arm long and place the end in a nostril and draw through it; in the other end they put the powder, and it purges them completely".

Cohiba was also the term used by Indians in Haiti and Quisqueya, on the island Columbus called La Española; the Caribs of Martinique and Guadaloupe said *yoli,* and the Oyampi Indians of Brazil *petun.* The Aztecs called it *picietl* and the Guaranís *cumpai.*

According to some authors, the word "tobacco" was derived from the name of the island Tobago, though others refute this origin.

More than any other American plant, tobacco has been associated with myths from the northern part of the continent to the south, passing through the isthmus and the Caribbean. The mystery of the smoke offered up in propitiatory ceremonies by wizards and priests and the intoxication produced by tobacco or *cohiba* spawned the myths, legends and visions that dominated their spiritual world.

Among the Aztecs, during the Toxcatl festival, a young man, the slimmest and handsomest of the prisoners, was feted for a year as the "god of gods" or Tezcatlipoca. During this period he received careful training worthy of a prince, learned to play the flute and sniff with elegance the perfume of flowers and the aroma of tobacco, which he smoked. Finally, he was led by canoe to the other side of the lake, to a small pyramid-shaped temple; as he climbed the pyramid he would strike his

6

7. Covering the fields with protective cloth.

7

8. Germinated seedbeds.

8

flute against each step. Once at the apex, he was laid down on a stone, and his heart was ripped out by the priests and offered to the Sun; his body was then carried down to the base of the temple and there its head was cut off and displayed on a pike.

Tlaloc, the Aztec rain god, sent puffs of smoke up to the firmament to create the clouds that generated celestial water. Ciacoatl, goddess of the earth, attired her divine body in fragrant tobacco leaves.

The goddess Cinacuati, or snake woman of the Aztecs, was identified with a grass called *picietl* or *tobaco*.

For the Winnebago Indians of North America, tobacco was a gift from the gods to the first human being; tossed into the fire, it propitiated the invocations the spirits raised to the heavens. The Senecas, an Indian tribe in what is now western New York State, believed that tabacco had sprung forth from the head of the daughter of the heavens, to be sprinkled on her tomb by her eldest son. The celestial mother added other gifts to this fructification: maize was born of her breasts, calabash from her womb, fava beans from her hands and the potato from her feet.

The Chippewas, in their sacred rites, before smoking their pipes, used to face the four cardinal points, each associated with a god. One of them, the god of the South, propitiated maize, melons and tobacco for man. They proffered its smoke to the thunder, the voice of the spirits.

For the Ojibwas, winter, represented by an old man with frozen face, was visited by a young man, the symbol of spring. During the night both smoked a pipe of tobacco mixed with aromatic herbs and recounted their deeds. At dawn, the old man had disappeared, transformed into water.

The Indians of Virginia so esteemed the tobacco plant that they considered it a special creation of the gods.

They burned it so the fragrant smoke would ascend, and when the rainstorms broke out, midst chanting and dancing, they threw handfuls of powdered tobacco into the air. The mythology of the Susquehanna tribes, described by North American patrician Benjamin Franklin, stated that the tobacco plant had germinated from the earth together with maize and kidney beans, thanks to the action of a youth who descended from the clouds and after tasting the roast tongue of a deer, prepared by some hunters, wished to reward them: "Come to this place at the thirteenth moon and you will find your recompense".

Tobacco, along with other plant species, was part of an unusual rite of the Creek Indians: they placed these offerings on an altar, covered them with clay and stacked branches on top. After two days of fasting, they set fire to the pile. The smoke and the flames that rose to the sky propitiated foregiveness for all sins committed, except murder.

One of the earliest historians of the Indies, Pedro Mártir de Anglería, tells us about the use of tobacco by the Antillean Indians, who to consult their idols or relics "inhaled *cohiba*, as they call the plant that produces rapture of the soul", and fallen into lethargy, as in a dream, they recounted what the divine images had communicated to them. According to Fray Bartolomé de las Casas, the aborigines sucked dark powders through straws, which produced the effect of a strong wine and left them "drunk or almost drunk. These powders and the ceremonies or acts were called *cohiba*".

The legends and miths of the Tainos mention the *cohiba* that Ayamanaco or Bayamanicoel loaded on Caracaracol's back in place of the bread he had requested. This caused an enormous swelling, and when his brothers cut into it with a stone axe, a live turtle sprang from the wound. Cuban ethnologist Fernando Ortiz compares the

10. *Biological check-up on the seedbeds.*

10

myth of Eve, who was born of a man's rib, with the legend of Caracaracol and points out that the powder of *cohiba* might represent erotism, which engendered a turtle, a generative symbol, on Caracaracol's back.

On the subject of the Cuban Indians and their tobacco, Ortiz tells us in his *Contrapunteo cubano del tabaco y el azúcar (Cuba Counterpoint of Tobacco and Sugar): Tobacco was the Indian's inseparable companion. From birth to death, the Indian lived wrapped in the spiraling smoke of tobacco, like the silk-cotton he squeezed for its fibers...*

In the Indian village, tobacco was part of its mythology, its religion, its magic, its medicine, its tribal ceremonies, its politics, its wars, its farming, its fishing, its collective stimulation, its public and private customs.

The wizards and soothsayers of the Venezuelan tribes consulted the demons and obtained their response from the way the broad tobacco leaves curled up when burned: if the fishing was to be good, the hunting successful, or even if a man was cruel to his wife.

In the mythology of the primitive tribes of Colombia, tobacco represented a human being. For their part, the healers of the Guajiro Indians were initiated into their order by chewing tobacco paste for several days, until they fell into ecstasy and thus performed acts of soothsaying and predestination of death.

The Jivaro Indians of the Amazonian basin initiated their youths, at the age of virility with the Kusupani feast, in which they smoked tobacco.

American Indian myths were quick to pass over to the lands of Africa, after the voyages of Columbus and his followers: the Bantus considered the tobacco spirit masculine, and so only men could cultivate it.

The sorcerers of Uganda also enjoy smoking tobacco in pipes until they fall into ecstasy.

11. Removal of the seedlings.

11

12/13. Transplanting a seedling.

12

13

Tobacco as a primitive medicine

The American Indians make multiple use of tobacco: they not only smoke it, they eat it, chew it, inhale it, lick it and drink it.
Examples of this are the Aracunas of Brazil, a strong, vigorous people who not only smoke the leaf but also ingest it as part of their diet. In Colombia, the Huitotos consume tobacco juice mixed with yucca juice, smoke it alone or wrapped in dried plantain leaves and, in ceremonies that sometimes last all night, they lick it from a gourd mixed with water and ashes; the Siones smoke it and lick or drink a very thick extract of it, to which they add various types of plant ashes; the Kogis, Ikas and Sankas prepare a concentrated paste which they rub on their teeth and gums and the Tucanos of Vuapés, among others, smoke large cigars wrapped in various leaves, such as plantain or maize, as well as tree bark; the Paeces apply it chewed to stop hemorrhages. Tobacco pastes and juices are highly concentrated and produce a strong reaction in those who consume them, such as stupefaction, lowering of body temperaure and perspiration.

The tradition of using tobacco as a medicinal plant has been widespread in America since remote times. The Aztecs mixed the leaf with lime, lanced tumors in a cross pattern and applied this mixture to "abcessess and growths". They also used it as an antidote for snake venom: after sucking the area of the bite, they applied heat and ground tobacco.

Pregnant women placed *picietl* or tobacco leaves on their breasts to free their children of illness. The Maya of Guatemala used tobacco leaves to make their wounds scar over. This custom of healing with tobacco leaves was later adopted by the Europeans. In the 16th century, the presumed knowledge of their medicinal properties, acquired from the Peruvian Indians by the Canarian monk Carmona, converted Pope Gregory XIII into a sincere admirer of tobacco.

His Holiness was ill, and no physician in Europe could give him hope of recovery. History recounts that Carmona healed him by applying tobacco.

During the reign of John III in Portugal, in that same century, tobacco was used against scabies, toothache, migraines, in lavages and as a scarring agent.

There is a vast bibliography concerning tobacco and medicine, so we shall mention only a few works on the subject.

Nicolás Monardes, born in Seville in 1512, considered the author of the first book on this plant, popularized "the great virtues and marvelous effects of the tobacco plant". The first part of his work has published in 1665 and then completed later, in 1754, with the title *First, Second and Third Part of Medicinal History and Things Derived from our West Indies which Serve as Medicines.*

Bernabé Cobo (1572-1659), Spanish Jesuit who authored the *History of the New World,* reported that tobacco was used "to treat innumerable maladies, applied as a fresh or dried leaf, in powdered form, as smoke, as a decoction and in other ways".

It was precisely in the 16th century that this appreciated leaf was taken to France from Portuguese lands by Jean Nicot, who presented it to his queen, Catherine de' Medici. She become accustomed to taking it in powder form to alleviate her migraines, and a royal page was even healed of *noli me tangere,* a serious form of skin ulcerations.

In fact, one of the names by which tobacco was known in that country was "herb of the queen". Francesco Montani wrote the following in his *Letter on Tobacco:*
This plant arrived in Lisbon from Florida and was planted in the royal gardens; one day, while Jean Nicot, Ambassador from the French King, was strolling there, the guard gave him a cutting, which Nicot planted in his home and soon succeeded in making it multiply. Moved by some sort of empirical curiosity, he tested it on a cancer and, when the initial results were good, tried it on eight

14. Cultivating with draft animals.

14

or ten others with admirable healing effect. He then tried applying the juice and paste of this herb to sores of all types, wounds, scrofulas and fistulas, and in every case found his remedy infallible. Nicot's home became a beehive of activity, people came from all over to seek treatment from this minister; hence tobacco came to be called the Ambassador's herb...

The scientific name of the plant, *Nicotiana tabacum,* was derived from the name of Nicot.

The use of tobacco in pharmacopeia helped spread its fame worldwide.

Robert Cudell reported in *Das Buch vom Tabak (The Book on Tobacco)* that at the end of the 16th century it was being used in tinctures, cosmetics, pills, powders, syrups, lavages, ointments and other products and also to treat intestinal colic, cutaneous eruptions, bone fractures and in the treatment of epilepsy, asthma and the plague.

In 1626, Johann Neander, German physician, published his book *Tobaccology or the Description of Tobacco or Nicotiana from the Medical, Surgical and Pharmacological Standpoints: Its Practical Application Against All Maladies of the Body and a Classification of all the Different Classes of Tobacco and their Corresponding Applications.*

A Persian ordinance of 1635 stated: "The sale of tobacco by anyone other than pharmacists shall be prohibited".

Esteban Pichardo, eminent Cuban geographer, referred in 1836 to the curative aspects of tobacco. In his *Diccionario provincial de voces cubanas (Provincial Dictionary of Cuban Terms)* he wrote: Tobaco *or, better said,* Cojiba, *its use now extended universally, is not just a pleasure that all the senses wish to enjoy, because in Spain and France they take it in with the nose, the Dutch, British and Anglo-Americans chew it; the Turks burn it in their pipes; the Africans, unhappy slaves, find some solace in their Cachimbo and everyone smokes it; it is* also a singularly effective remedy for tetanus or lockjaw, so frequent in those climes, and in rubbing compounds; baths or lavages.

Our national hero José Martí, in his article "Tobacco" published in June 1884 in *La America* (New York), reported some anecdotes on the medicinal properties of this plant, related by General Chingman of North Carolina.

This soldier was wounded by a ball in the leg, below the kneecap, and was healed by applying tobacco leaves to it. On another occasion, during an attack of sciatica, "moistened tobacco leaves were placed on the hip, and the pain disappeared". Martí adds: *The first he saw fifty years ago was a Cuban peasant who treated the inflamed eyes of his draft horse with tobacco juice; and later, in lands where they suffer a great deal from irritation of the eyelids, he saw that the people were cured of it with extreme facility by simply sleeping one night or more with a moistened tobacco leaf covering the eyelids.*

The Laplanders of Sweden apply tobacco ash as a tonic to avoid baldness and to regain lost hair. In the Netherlands, until a few years ago, tobacco leaves were used to alleviate toothache.

Finally, let us close this chapter with the opinion of Cuban botanist Juan Tomás Roig, who in his *Diccionario (...)* declared that tobacco is "a medicinal plant; it is narcotic, purgative and antiparasitic. It is commonly used as an insecticide, in decoctions. Its active principle is nicotine, which is used as an antitetanic and against paralysis of the bladder, in a dosage of 1 to 10 drops. It is also used in injections".

Wild tobacco *(Nicotinana glauca Graham),* a wild plant which grows chiefly on the coast, is still used for medicinal purposes by some peasants. Its leaves are used: in decoction, against hemorrhoids; in poultices, to alleviate rheumatic pain; and moistened with saliva, to heal sores, inflammation and burns.

15. Cultivating with draft animals.

15

16. Manual cultivation: Guataquea.

16

17. Hanging the protective cloth.

Amazon to Caribbean by canoe

It is always interesting to verify in the field what we have read in books. Our opportunity to travel through the rivers and forests of South America came in 1987, during the expedition "From Amazon to Caribbean by Canoe", made for the purpose of re-enacting how the Caribbean Sea could have been discovered by prehistoric tribes from the Amazon and Orinoco basins.

Among a host of other things, we were able to learn, live and direct, as we say today, the curative methods still practiced by some South American tribes with tobacco, as well as their mythologies associated with the aromatic leaf.

On 6 March, after our canoes had left behind the villages of the upper Rio Napo, a tributary of the Amazon, we visited a hut occupied by Quichua Indians, not far from the river port of Francisco de Orellana, in Ecuador. Those aborigines were terrified: a poisonous snake had bitten a young man in the family. They immediately reached for tobacco stored in rolls; one of them chewed the tobacco to his mouth and then applied the plug to the wound produced by the serpent's fangs.

On 23 March, we reached the confluence of the Santa Maria and Napo rivers and canoed up that affluent to establish contact with the Secoya Indians, whose houses stood on the high river bank. Curivari, chief of the clan, dressed in a long green sarong, spoke a few words of Spanish, and with the help of our Quichua guide informed us about their customs and the tragedy of his tribe, how year after year it was being decimated by the ruthless encounter of so-called civilization.

While we conversed, Curivari reached for a *monto*, a roll of tobacco tightly wrapped from end to end by plant fiber, similar to a large stick of dynamite. He cut off a round slice and explained that he chewed it to regain the strength he lost during long hikes in the forest.

On 31 March, proceeding down the Napo, we came to the brook or small river of Urco Mirano, where we visited a hamlet of Yagua Indians, settled on barren hills contrasting with the surrounding thick forest. The 23 houses built entirely of forest materials accomodated 203 inhabitants.

Maximo Cahuachi, young promoter of the community's health, told us: "Snake venom comes from the cold. All illnesses come from the cold and excessive heat. Tobacco serves against snakebite. It is mixed with water, it is pounded and after it has been well chewed it is placed on the wound. We also use the juice of a plant called *piripiri,* which is soaked or boiled in water".

In Leticia, a Colombian settlement on the banks of the Amazon, we learned of the myth of the Moainame tribe. Its members use drugs to enter the realm of their myths and learn of their past. They consider their lands at La Chorrera the center of the Universe, the birthplace of humanity. They recount that after a deluge of hot water, men and animals were changed into stone, and the few survivors were left imprisoned in the subsoil; one day God the creator decided to extricate them. To do so, he planted maize so that they could climb up its roots to the surface; when this attempt failed, he planted tobacco for the same purpose.

Also on the Orinoco River we learned that many of its inhabitants still use tobacco leaves to heal some of their ills and explain by means of myths the portentous events of the creation of man and the world that surrounds us.

The leaf that provoked so many dreams still maintains its hold over the primitive world of the American forest.

18. Developing tobacco plant.

18

19. *Sucker and bud removal.*
20. *Bud removal.*

19

Inquisition, anathemas and bulls against smokers

The first European to try the delicious leaf was that same Rodrigo de Xerez who saw the Cuban Indians smoking along the paths of the fief of Maniabón. Once back in his native land of Ayamonte, according to C. Corti, he was discovered in his house blowing smoke from his mouth, an exceptional sight in feudal Spain. Mistaking this for a case of demon possession, the Holy Service sent him to expiate his "sin" in a dungeon.

Freed years later, Rodrigo saw that many neighbors in Ayamonte had begun smoking the "bedeviled leaf".

In a royal patent of 16 September 1586, Philip II put teeth into the superstitions circulating about the "intrinsic evil" of the leaf by imposing a punishment of whipping and exile on its growers and sellers, and ordered that it "be publicly burned as a harmful and damaging herb".

Kings and the popes and priests of Christ and Mohammed set out to dissuade their subjects and faithful from acquiring a taste for tobacco.

Shah 'Abbas I the Great of Persia, who began his reign in 1588, condemned to death all those who used tobacco in any form.

The anathema against tobacco issued by English King James I in 1604 epitomized that traditional Euroecentrism according to which everything that came from the overseas colonies was to be scorned. Let us read:

Since this plant, which is a common herb that, under various name, grows almost everywhere, was first discovered and used by some barbarian indios *as a preservative and an antidote against pustules, loathsome malady to which these savages are, as we all know, very exposed, due to the filthy and browned constitution of their bodies and the excessive heat of their climate; so that when*

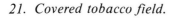

21. Covered tobacco field.

these peoples were first brought to Christianity, with them came this extremely loathsome ailment accompanied by the habit of tobacco, *used as a foul and bitter antidote for such an execrable and putrid ill and hedonistic fumigation, still in use by them against it, as though they expected to heal one poison with another.*

In Japan, as in other countries, tobacco was prohibited. In 1907, the shogun of Tokugawa sentenced smokers, among other punishments, to confiscation of their property and fifty days of imprisonment.

The Moslem hierarchy lost no time in proclaiming that the use of both tobacco and coffee were against their sacred book, the Koran, and that practitioners of said delights would have their heads lopped off. Murad IV, sultan of Turkey, who began his reign in 1622, punished smokers by cutting off their noses and ears.

Pope Urban VIII issued a bull in 1624 in which he stated:

Not long ago we were informed that the evil habit of taking the herb vulgarly known as tabaco *by mounth and nostrils has totally spread throughout many dioceses, to the extent that persons of both sexes, and even priests and clerics, both secular and regular, forgetting the decorum befitting their rank, consume it everywhere, and principally in the temples of the town and diocese of Hispale (Seville), feeling no shame, during the celebration of the very holy ordinance of the mass, soiling the sacred vestments with the repugnant humors that tobacco causes, infesting the temples with a repellent odor — to the great scandal of their brethren who keep to the righteous path — and seeming not to fear the irreverence of things holy in the least.*

In conclusion, the pope declares:

...by means of this document, let us place in interdiction and prohibit as a consequence, all collectively and each individually, of both sexes, laymen, ecclesiastics, all the religious orders and those belonging to any institution of said nature, from consuming tabaco *under the porticos and in the interior of the churches, whether it be chewed, smoked in a pipe and sniffed as powder into the nose; in other words, from using it in any form. Anyone violating theese provisions shall be promptly excommunicated,* ipso facto, *no more no less, in accordance with the terms of this interdiction.*

In 1635, in Spain, Fray Tomás Ramón opposed the use of tobacco, invoking the name of God, a rejection which was maintained with fluctuations until 1725.

In 1645, Czar Alexander of Russia ordered all smokers deported to the cold lands of Siberia, and later issued another decree imposing torture and even death. The tobaccophobia of the Russian aristocracy ended when Peter the Great, who grew fond of consuming the leaf during a trip to England, legalized smoking and also arranged for it to benefit the Czarist treasury: in 1697 the Russian monarchy established a tobacco monopoly in Siberia.

The categorical order of Oliver Cromwell to his troops to rip up tobacco plants and punish smokers implacably failed to slow down the expansion of the smoking habit to any extent.

Laws were enacted against smokers until 1921. The U.S. State of Kansas approved one that was later repealed because, as in earlier centuries, the people ignored it. The same thing happened in Illinois.

22

Why do we smoke?

For a wide range of reasons, almost all of a psychological nature. We smoke to release nervous tension. Workers of all classes smoke while they toil. Other times, at intervals, to distract our attention and focus it anew with greater intensity. For many workers, rest periods tend to be of uniform length: the duration of a cigarette. Rest is more complete because our attention is more diverted or distracted while we are smoking a cigarette or consuming a pipeful.

This is how Salvador Massip replies in his article "The Economic Geography of Tobacco". He also affirms: "There is probably no habit as wide-spread among men and women of all races, all cultural levels and all social conditions".

From these psychological standpoints, we should examine more thoroughly why smoking is so universal and study why the world consumes billions of cigarettes and hundreds of millions of cigars each year. On the subject of habits, it is a singular fact that so many people in the world need to occupy their mouths with so many different materials; chewing gum, pipe or cigarette holder, tobacco, cigarettes and candies, including the ghastly habit of drugs.

In the East they use hashish, or cannabis indica, as well as opium; hashish, which is mixed with tobacco and smoked in a pipe, produces the effect of a drug that generates a form of true madness. Some peoples smoke the leaves of tomato, potato and *tucílago* plants, the last type against colds. In the Alps there is a plant, popularly called "mountain tobacco", that some Swiss consume and that affects the heart and is thus poisonous. Some North American Indians smoke the dried leaves of a type of holly, which produces a stupor and strange visions, and the narcotic *lobelia* leaf, both in pipes. A similar species is used in Siberia, where the leaves are smoked moistened. The Bahamians smoke cascarilla bark. In Africa, the Kaffirs use camphor leaves, which produces aphasia or loss of the power of speech; the Hottentots, in particular, smoke dagga.

With regard to tobacco, it is well to remember that not all types contain the same level of nicotine. This specific alkaloid is found in distinct profusion in the tobaccos of France and Germany; in Virginia and Kentucky there is less; Paraguayan tobacco is similar; in Sumatra it is a little lower; Braziian, Hungarian, Philippine, Javanese, Dominican and Puerto Rican types vary from 3 to 2,25% while Havana cigar leaves contain even less of this alkaloid, though it varies with the class.

Martí also wrote on the subject of health, cigarettes and tobacco in an article published in *La América* (New York) in September 1883: "We have nothing to say against smoking at the appropriate times and in moderation (...)".

On 29 April 1921 a tobacco exhibition was held in London, at which the eminent British physician Sir James Cantlie affirmed that there were four social poisons: "tea, coffee, tobacco and alcohol, and of the four, tobacco is the one which causes less damage".

24

25. *The* veguero *(tobacco-grower) contemplating his work, the leaves cultivated under cheesecloth are the finest, most exclusive product of tobacco farming production.*

26. *Walking in a covered tobacco plantation.*

25

26

The art of smoking

Smokers in history

For millions of human beings, smoking is a pleasure, but it has rules.

So we do not believe we are exaggerating if we say that it is an art born of a rite, and each of us uses it in his own way.

The first act of a smoker is to select his cigar; then he cuts the tip, a delicate act that can ensure proper draw. Some leave on the band, others remove it. In reality, if too tight, it may break the smooth wrapper leaf.

A cigar must be lit with a short, hot, odorless flame; wax-coated matches and fluid lighters should be avoided. The flame must be held one centimeter below the end of the cigar and the cigar rotated until it is completely lit.

It is difficult to express a judgement about the taste of tobacco. Its "flavour" is savored by both tasting and smelling. Taste and odour are closely united and are the result of the properties of the raw material that forms this particular product.

The smoker manifests his elegance as soon as he brings the cigar to his lips. His smooth, delicate gestures, the enjoyment with which he contemplates the capricious forms the smoke assumes in the air, denote a man who knows the art of smoking.

In his article "Manual on the Venezuelan Tobacco-grower", José Martí says that tobacco is "...the india leaf, comfort of the pensive, delight of the daydreamer, fragrant bosom of the winged opal (...). Perhaps smokers are right: it is sometimes better to watch tobacco smoke drawing lions and eagles in the air than to feel them, as spiritual smoke, go to our heads!"

Frederick I the Great of Prussia (1712-1786) was among the sovereigns most enthusiastic about smoking.

Napoleon Bonaparte (1769-1821) inhaled snuff and smoked cigars with an elegance recorded by history. "One could always tell where the French Emperor had stopped a few moments by the quantity of tobacco strewn on the floor", as we read in the article "Napoleon Bonaparte, Benefactor of Tobacco".

One of the great smokers of history was Abraham Lincoln (1809-1865). He liked corncob and clay pipes, which he packed with the cut tobacco grown in the United States, but when he tried the aromatic Havana cigars, he was enthused by them. And the man famed for abolishing slavery in the United States also chewed tobacco.

Martí said that Benito Juárez (1806-1872) was the cigar smoker "who tossed an empire into the sea and was able to defy poverty with honour and recaptured and ensured the independence of his country!"

United States General and President Ulysses Grant (1822-1885) smoked 20 to 25 cigars a day.

Polish Marshall Jozéf Pilsudski (1867-1935), inveterate smoker, declared: "I shall never be separated from the friend who helped me spend the most enjoyable moments of my life".

During World War II, fought by the allies against Nazi-Fascism, it was a well-known fact that the Big Three — Stalin, Roosevelt and Churchill — were smokers of pipe, cigarette and Havana cigar, respectively. Churchill

27. *Transporting harvested leaves in a basket.*

27

made famous the phrase: "I always hold Cuba in my mouth".

Ernesto Che Guevara recounted how he was won over by the aroma of Havana cigars in the rebel camps of the Sierra Maestra: "An habitual and extremely important complement in the life of a guerrilla is smoking, whether cigarettes, cigars or pipe tobacco, for the smoke that he can expel in moments of relaxation is a great companion to the lonely soldier".

The inspiring spirals of smoke have accompanied significant scientific discoveries in recent centuries.

Isaac Newton (1642-1727) was smoking when he saw the famous apple fall that led him to discover the law of universal gravity. Another Englishman, Charles Darwin (1809-1882), wrote his theories on natural selection and the origin of man enveloped in the smoke of his cigarettes.

Paul Ehrlich (1854-1915), German biologist, disciple of Robert Koch and discover of Salvarsan (606), an anti-syphillis arsenic compound, was an elegant smoker and often affirmed: "I can't think without smoking. Tobacco stimulates me".

Elsa Einstein, wife of physics genius Albert Einstein (1879-1955), said that her husband "emits smoke like a chimney when he is engrossed in his thoughts" and added that her husband smoked a long, straight pipe that he always carried in his pocket, along with a pencil.

We can also cite examples of composers and singers.

The passion of Johann Sebastian Bach (1685-1750) for smoking inspired him to compose "The Tobacco Pipe".

Ludwig van Beethoven (1770-1827) always smoked in the tavern, never on the street or at home.

Richard Wagner (1813-1883) told a Viennese that bestowed some Havana cigars on him: "You have unquestionably helped in my opera *"Die Götterdämmerung.* This

morning these marvels from Havana arrived and they immediately transported me to such enchantment as Pythis must have felt when he was enveloped in the vapours of Apollo".

Enrico Caruso (1873-1921), famous opera singer, had included in all the contracts he signed "the right to smoke on any part of the stage from the moment the curtain rises". Hipólito Lázaro (1889-1965), famous Spanish tenor, also enjoyed savoring our Havana cigars, and said as much in his autobiography.

Another *aficionado* of Havana cigars was Finnish composer Jean Sibelius (1865-1957). On his eighty-third birthday, he was given a fine box of cigars by our Comisión Nacional de Propaganda y Defensa del Tabaco Habano. In his thank-you note, Sibelius wrote: "Since one of my uncles lived and died in Cuba, I have always been greatly interested in your admirable country. Moreover, I have smoked Havana cigars all my life and, of course, they have always been highly meaningful for me".

28

The world's best tobacco

French botanist Joseph P. de Tournefort (1656-1708) established the classification of tobacco, also adopted by Linneas, though he later eliminated some plants from it.
Famed Cuban scholar Juan Tomás Roig y Mesa, in his *Diccionario Botánico de nombres vulgares cubanos (Botanical Dictionary of Common Cuban Names)* explains that tobacco, *Nicotiana tabacum,* of the solanacea family, is a plant native to South America, an annual herb around two meters tall, with an erect stalk and numerous large leaves, oblong and lanceolate, measuring up to 30 centimeters in length; purplish or pink flowers, with a yellowish or greenish sheath and a tubulous, bell-shaped calyx.
Of the varieties of *Nicotiana tabacum,* the finest is the one known by the scientific name *havenensis,* cultivated almost exclusively in Cuba.
The name wild tobacco is applied to numerous wild species with leaves that, according to a scientific account, "more or less resemble those of tobacco. The Solanaceae include *Nicotiana plumbaginifolia* Viv., *N. repanda* Willdl, *Solanum verbascifolium* Lin., *S. Antillarum* O.E. Schulz; *Schwenkia americana* Lin. The Loganiaceas include *Buddleia americana* Lin., and the Hidroleaceas the *Nama spinosa* (L.), J. Kuntze".
On his visit to Cuba at the beginning of the last century. Alexander von Humboldt wrote in the fourth chapter of his book *Political Essay on the Island of Cuba:* "The tobacco of the island of Cuba is famous in all the parts of Europe where it is smoked". He added: "Though the tobacco of Vuelta Abajo is the most famous, the type produced in the eastern part of the island is also heavily exported".

29

29. Preparation of drying frames for sungrown tobacco on lath.

*30. Gathering and transporting the harvested leaf.
Threaded sungrown tobacco.*

"Its classic homeland is the island of Cuba, primarily the Havana tobacco of Vueltabajo, which is without rival in the world", Esteban Pichardo tells us in his *Diccionario provincial de voces cubanas.*
"The best species is that of Cuba, known by the name of Havana tobacco", affirms Antonio Blanco Fernández, physician and surgeon, in his *Manual de agricultura,* 1868.
The tobacco produced in Cuba has always enjoyed universal fame.
In his book *Half a Century of Tobacco,* Morton R. Edwin wrote these words: "Up to the present there can be no question that the tobacco of Cuba is the aristocrat of its class. For cigar smokers in all the world, there is something magical, a special enchantment associated with the words Cuba and Havana, when they are associated with the idea of fine tobacco".
And he adds: "...though all nations made rapid advances in the cultivation of tobacco, which permitted and stimulated the development of the new industry, the island of Cuba succeeded in producing the crops of the best tobacco in the world, though it should be noted that America produces the finest varieties known on the market".
The *Encyclopaedia Britannica* affirms: "Cuban tobacco has long been recognized superior in terms of flavour and aroma;" for its part, the *Encyclopaedia Americana* says that in the western part of Cuba "they cultivate the world's best tobacco, as its exquisite and extraordinary aroma is known to all".
In 1912, referring to the qualities of our tobacco, North American Maximillian Stern, of the Committee of Importers and Manufacturers, declared: "Tobacco of the same quality as Havana cannot be grown in the United States. The many experiments conduced using seed from Cuba, alone and mixed with local varieties, have failed to give satisfactory results. Havana tobacco is unique in its aroma, and no other has been remotely able to imitate it, nor can it be used successfully as a substitute for it".
The Federal Trade Commission, reporting in 1928 on the Havana cigar, repeats the concepts of the Attorney Commissions:
Due to its characteristics aroma and delicate flavour, Cuban tobacco has been considered (...) the best in the world for the manufacturing of cigars; and, as a consequence, cigars made with that exquisite tobacco enjoy the reputation as a unique product among smokers and in commerce. This reputation has existed for over 300 years, and no other tobacco has ever surpassed it or even equalled it.
Many cigars manufactured in other countries of the world, to be accepted by discerning smokers, contain at least a part of Cuban leaves.
Hence the declaration of Olcott F. King, official of the U.S. Department of Agriculture, who affirmed in February 1938: "We never consider a cigar good unless it contains filler from Cuba".

The Havana cigar
and geography

Havana tobacco is the favoured child of Cuban agricolture, thanks to the combination of extraordinary geographical factors and the expert, pains-taking efforts of our agricultural and industrial workers, which have favoured our unparalleled leaf. The climate of Cuba, a fundamental factor in excellent tobacco growing, is the consequence of its geographical location, very near the Tropic of Cancer and distant from the rigours of the Equator.

The Havana's homeland covers 110,860 square kilometers, a figure that includes the island of Cuba, the island of Juventad and up to 4,195 other islets and cays. Its total population is just over ten million.

The average annual temperature is 25° Celsius; record lows and highs of 1°C and 40°C have been recorded. The average relative humidity is 79%.

Average annual rainfall varies, according to the region, from 3,400 millimeters in the northeastern (and over 5,000 mm in extremely rainy years) to 600 mm in the southeast (with minimums in dry years below 200 mm). In the Sierra de los Organos, where lofty peaks enclose beautiful valleys planted in tobacco, an average of 2,000 mm falls per year, but in the south of Pinar del Río province it does not exceed 1,000 mm.

As far as barometric pressure is concerned, the annual variation is rather small, from maximums of around 1,109 millibars in January and February to minimums around 1014 millibars in October.

Although the seasons vary little, they undoubtedly influence the agricultural and processing cycle of tobacco. In spring the leaves are cured and at season's end they are bundled and stacked for fermentation. During this season and into the summer, the fertile tobacco fields are left fallow to permit their enrichment with organic materials for the next crop. At the end of summer, the land is tilled to aid the decomposition of buried plant matter and increase soil fertility. In autumn, the preparation of tobacco lands is intensified and at the end of this season the seedlings are planted; the tobacco is then harvested in winter.

Since time immemorial, it has been said that the land of Cuba produces the best tobacco in the world. In 1822, José Fernández de Madrid described the different geographical regions devoted to the growing of tobacco:

The high, rocky cachimbo *lands (casimbas) usually give the best pipe tobacco. The same occurs in the low-lying, light, sandy soils, located chiefly along the riverbanks, and in valleys that receive water of nearby hills and mountains. Such are the lands in the districts of the* vuelta de abajo, *which certainly give a superior tobacco (...) the determination and esteem with which consumers sought to buy for all these many years is evident proof that it deserves (...). The* vuelta de abajo *is the land included between the Guanacage ranch to the cape of San Antonio. The poor, sandy soil of those flatlands, so inhospitable for other crops, produces the mildest, most delicate pipe tobacco. The avenues of the rivers that descend from the mountains toward the northern coast, with their deposits, bring fertility to the banks and form natural tobacco plantations worthy of their fame. But however much these lands of the* vuelta de abajo *have been praised, do not think they derived from nature the exclusive right to produce mild pipe tobacco, because throughout the island, along the banks of its many rivers, we may find fertile lowlands more or less suitable for the purpose. This is the case, for example, of the bright red soils found at Virtudes, Canoa, Jiaraco, Candela, Guanajo, Cármen, Zábalo and Zaragoza. The thick, rich black soil gives the tobacco with large, tough leaves of the perfect quality for snuff, but it can also serve as pipe tobacco after enough time has passed for it to weaken a little. The lands of the Güines are of this type, including Babajagua, Bacima, San Pedro, San Julian, Lechuga, Melena, Buey-Sabana and others, although there are also soils in these areas suitable for growing mild pipe tobacco.*

Today, pedological science, the study of the various soils in the country, explains their chemical characteristics and agricultural properties.

Thus the tobacco-growing area that takes in much of Havana province, where high quality wrapper leaf is grown, is composed of reddish soils, technically classified as latosols, and also tropical reds, ferralites and laterites or brick-reds, deposited on the calcites of the Miocene period and formed by clay loam with minute quartz particles and little organic material, slightly acid pH, sometimes with occasional buckshot and concretions of iron. The combination of these soils and the specific climate of the area forms the natural base for producing the exqisiteness of our Havana cigars.

The tobacco-growing soils of San Juan y Martínez and San Luis, "the heart of the famous Vuelta Abajo tobacco area", according to the apt phrase of U.S. soil experts Bennett and Allison, serve as a basis for cultivating tobacco of the highest quality. In general, they are classified as sandy, quartzitic and ferruginous soils deposited on rocks of the Lower and Middle Jurassic.

In the karstic intermontane valleys, such as Viñales, we find residual soils that originated from the decomposition of the clayey shales that form the structure of the hills opposite the mountainous slopes of Los Organos. These soils contain much quartz particulate, among other elements.

Near the center of Cuba, in the area of Manicaragua, the soils are tropical dun-colored, deposited on acid rocks like plagiogranite of the Upper Cretaceous period, and allow intense tobacco planting because they are also formed of dun-colored

sandy loam with a subangular granule structure.

The Spanish brought in African blacks to work in the sugar industry and promoted the immigration of whites, principally from the Canary Islands, for lucrative tobacco growing.

Nonetheless, in the 17th century Cuba was almost deserted, and it was necessary to populate those empty spaces:

...to all those who came to request tobacco lands, they were granted for an insignificant yearly rent, and often without any rent at all, for the sole purpose of attributing, with their residence, some life and movement to localities deserted and almost unknown until then. In this way they promoted the cultivation of tobacco, which offered manifest advantages for developing the white population and agricultural welath, when on 15 October 1659, on petition from the municipal council of Trinidad, the Governor of Havana ordered that all the lowlands washed by the waters of the Agabama, Arimaoa and Caracusey rivers be set aside for rural exploitation,

says Jacobo de la Pezuela in his *Diccionario geográfico estadístico e histórico de la Isla de Cuba (Statistical and Historical Atlas of the Island of Cuba).*

Later the planting of tobacco was extended to the lowlands of Havana, and the first plantations were established at Jesús del Monte and Santiago de las Vegas. Thus the producers could trade directly with the ships that visited the port of Havana.

In the early 18th century, the Spanish monarchy instituted *Estanco* (monopoly), which obliged the tobacco farmers to sell tobacco solely to the government at fixed prices. All the crude tobacco thus acquired was processed in Seville.

In 1772, the Governor of the island, Don Felipe de Fondesviela, Marquis de la Torre, appointed Juan Varca to establish jurisdiction over Nueva Filipina (Pinar del

31

32

Río), precisely because of the economic importance of the tobacco produced there, since its cultivation has been initiated in Los Hoyos del Cuyagúateje. Later, its cultivation was extended to the area traditionally known as the hills and plains of Vueltabajo.

The tobacco growing boom in Cuba favored the founding of various cities, one of which was the Habanera town of Bejucal, originally composed of thirty tobacco-farming families. Later, an entire province, Pinar del Río, was populated by farming villages and towns thanks to the intense growing of tobacco, which proved to be the best quality in the area of the Havana cigar. In 1827 there were 5,500 tobacco plantations; by 1859 this number had grown to 9,500. In this same period there were around 1,300 cigar factories in Havana and more than 20 cigarette plants. This prosperity was due to the large volume of Cuban exports to the United States, but in 1857 that nation erected tariff barriers and a crisis followed.

Since colonial time, the following five tobacco-growing districts have been known: Vuelta Abajo Zone; Semivuelta Zone; Partido Zone; Remedios or Vuelta Arriba Zone and Oriente Zone.

The Vuelta Abajo Zone includes almost all the province of Pinar del Río, except the southern section, occupied by what is called the Semivuelta.

The tobacco coming from this region is employed in the production of high-quality cigars. Vuelta Abajo is divided in turn into five subzones: Llano includes San Juan y Martínez and San Luis; Lomas designates the area of tobacco growing in the shaley hills of Pinar del Río, the famous adjoining valleys such as Viñales, part of Guane and San Juan y Martínez; Remates y Guane includes parts of Guane, in its limits with the Guanahacabibes Peninsula; Costa Norte embraces the northern part of the province,

Mantua, Pinar del Río, part of Viñales and Consolación del Norte; Costa Sur includes the areas of San Luis, Pinar del Río and Consolación del Sur.

The Semivuelta area is the second tobacco-growing region of Pinar del Río and is composed of Consolacion del Sur, Candelaria, Los Palacios and San Cristóbal; its tobacco, with thick leaves and aroma stronger than that grown in Vuelta Abajo, was once exported to the North American market and the domestic cigar industry.

The Partido area includes the communities of San Antonio de los Baños, Güira del Melena and Alquízar, in the province of Havana. In this zone as in the Pinareño towns of San Juan y Martínez and San Luis, the tobacco is grown under cheesecloth; this covering enables growers to obtain lighter leaves with smoother texture, used to manufacture the luxury cigars for export.

The Remedios area, also called Vuelta Arriba, includes almost all the province of Las Villas. It is one of Cuba's richest tobacco-growing regions. Its leaf is thick and aromatic.

The last of the areas is the Oriente, which embraces the regions of Bayamo, Mayarí, Alto Songo, Jiguaní and Sagua de Tánamo, where tobacco is produced for local consumption and for supplying the cigar industry.

In the furrow

The agricultural phase of tobacco begins with the selection and preparation of the fields, which must have no steep slopes, to avoid the washing of the seed.

Once the seed is placed in the seedbed, it is covered with cloth or straw to protect it from the sun's rays, which can be harmful in this initial stage. After five to eight days, the tobacco begins to germinate, and two or three days later the covering is removed in the morning and after-noon, so the seedlings can gradually become used to their surroundings.

Ten to 12 days after planting, the periodic application of insecticides and fungicides begins, to halt the development of pests and disease.

After 35 days, in the second half of October, when the plants are around 15 centimeters tall, they are transplanted to the permanent fields; this land has already been improved with the application of calcium carbonate, organic fertilizer and other substances. Fertilization is repeated after ten and 20 days; then the work of cultivation and banking begins, with the objective of removing weeds and promoting the proper growth and development of the plants. Then insecticides are applied again.

This process was described poetically by Francisco Poveda (1796-1884) in his poem "To Cuba":

What can compare with the
Fertile tobacco fields of my Cuba?
Nothing.
At the foot of the leafy mountain
The seedbed is laid and the land
Is then prepared in lined furrows
Where the tender seedlings are transplanted
And covered as soon as they catch,
And then through care and efficiency
Lead the weak, fragile plantlets
Come to give off aromas that amber covets
And smooth to the touch, later transformed
Into the cigars of Havana.

Irrigation must be carefully regulated: too much or too little can cause irreparable damage, both in yield and quality, particularly during the harvesting stage. Currently the fertilizer used is of both chemical and organic origin (manure) or, in very rare cases, bat guano extracted from caves, used a great deal through the centuries in the tobacco fields, especially in Pinar del Río. In the article "Fertilizing Tobacco", published in the magazine *El Tabaco,* Havana, 25 May 1900, we read:

Throughout the mountain range that extends from Caimito de Guayabal, the border between Havana and Pinar del Río provinces, to Punta de la Sierra, a distance of over 50 leagues, there are an infinite number of caves in which flocks of bats and fowl have sought shelter since prehistoric times, and these caves have become large, perhaps limitless deposits of guano that should be analyzed thoroughly and carefully, because we may discover in this material a treasure for our agriculture, after we have sent such great quantities abroad to pay for fertilizers which were often found to be produced in Philadelphia and sold as the product of the caves of Lower Peru and the Pacific coast.

The perceptive eye of U.S. writer Samuel Hazard stresses the profound expertise of the Cuban *veguero* or tobacco grower to raise the excellent leaf, a task he performs like a virtuoso:

Guided by the results of long experience handed down by his ancestors, the farmer knows, without being able to explain it scientifically, the way to increase or decrease the strength or mildness of tobacco. His right hand, as though guided by instinct, knows which buds to remove to limit the development or growth of the plant or what may be necessary to do to leave only the best quality leaves.

But his principal task, to which he devotes most of the hours of his life, is the extermination of the voracious insects that attack the plant. One of these insects, called

34. *Predrying of threaded tobacco, under cloth.*

35. *Tobacco curing barn.*

the cutworm, chooses its home on the underside of the leaves; the green June beetle larva attacks the ends of the leaves; the grub eats away the heart of the plant and all cause some degree of damage.

The tobacco grower spends entire nights with lights, freeing the sprouting seedling of the destructive pests. But he fights an ever tougher battle against worse enemies, the bibijaguas *or destructive ants, a species of large ant, native to the country, which are to tobacco what the locust is to wheat.*

The tobacco grower has to care for each of his plants as though it "were a delicate maiden", to use the expression of José Martí.

The tobacco plant, according to its leaves, is divided into three parts: the corona, the center and the bottom, all of which are harvested.

When the leaves reach full development, buds appear. They draw their nourishment from substances in the leaves, so they must be removed, a process called *desbotonar* or debudding. The plant will strain to reproduce these offsprings or buds, which will also have to be eliminated, an operation the *vegueros* call *repasar,* i.e. removing suckers. The small buds, sometimes hidden among the large leaves, are considered by the farmers as "the disgrace of a good *veguero*".

Passing through the tobacco fields, the bud-remover observes the plants and with his thumbnail and index finger snips off the buds in a single motion to prevent damage. In this way the grower obtains a superior leaf, demostrate by its light green colour with tiny yellow-green spots, indicators that it is ready for cutting and the later fermentation process. The perfect leaves are selected as wrappers *(capas).*

Tobacco-grower Roberto Padilla, speaking of the *repasado* with journalist Ada Ormas, specialist on tobacco, affirmed: "These offspring are their mother's enemies because they drain her life, take her strength away, make her fall ill, and we must look after the mother's interests, for these are plants that give the finest wrapper leaves, the wrapper leaves of Vuelta Abajo".

For the harvest, important weather factors must be taken into account, such as the dry southern wind which withers the tobacco. When the moment comes to detach the leaf from the stock, it is pressed with the index finger and carefully removed with a single hand movement.

Those selected as wrappers, which must be stacked one on the other to form a bundle of 25, are called a *plancha* or hand.

The leaves are cut in six phases, called *libre de pie* (at the base), *uno y medio* (one-and-a-half), *centro ligero* (light center), *centro fino* (thin center), *centro gordo* (thick center) and *corona.* Wrappers can be cut only beginning with *uno y medio,* and the best yields are obtained with the center leaves.

The tobacco destined for wrappers, the fine outer covering of Havana cigars, requires special cultivation. To avoid excessive sunlight, it must grow under fine cloth covering: cheesecloth or *topada,* introduced by Luis Marx in the last century, which will also protect it from wind and disease.

Tobacco under *tapado* is classified as *ligero* (light), *seco* (dry), *viso* (glossy), *amarillo* (yellow), *medio tiempo* (half texture) and *quebrado* (broken), while the sungrown type is divided into *volado, seco, ligero,* and *medio tiempo.* The leaves are classified by size into large, average and small and by physical condition into healthy, broken and distressed.

When the harvest is over, expert workers on tall wooden stilts, like circus performers, take down the protective cheesecloths and put them away for the next planting.

34

35

The tobacco barn

The tobacco leaves, cut and bundled into *planchas*, change hands from the picker to the sacador, a worker also called a *hojero*. Then the *llenador* or packer places them delicately in groups of around 300 leaves into oval baskets and covers them with mosquito netting or sack-cloth for their trip to the tobacco barn.

Like the lofty gothic cathedrals, tobacco barns must be oriented according to the cardinal compass points, facing west so the sun will heat the front and the rear only in the early morning and late afternoon. They remain closed throughout the curing phase of the leaves.

The workers who care for the tobacco in these large barns must keep a close eye on the ambient temperature and humidity, as well as the rainfall, and open and close the doors as a consequence.

Many tobacco barns have been engineered and built of modern materials; likewise, some have been equipped with heaters to reduce curing time, but it is still common to see them in their original style, with thatched roofs of our royal palm fronds. One of the first tasks performed in the tobacco barn is stringing. This is generally done by women. Using large needles, the stringers must align the leaves and place them on long sticks called *cujes* which are raised onto the *barrederas,* horizontal boards where they rest on their ends. A good stringer can fill at least a hundred sticks in a day's work.

A *cuje* is a straight pole just over four meters long and thick on the two ends; it is highly useful in the long drying and curing process the tobacco must undergo for 45 or 60 days, according to climatic conditions. *Cujeros* are the workers responsible for cutting them. Not all regions offer sticks of quality; they must be selected in marshes or along sandless coastal areas and even in the thick mangrove swamps. The mangrove provides good *cujes* for tobacco.

Like all the operations in the agricultural and industrial process of tobacco, the *cuje* has a technology all its own: after cutting, it is kept in salt water for around 50 days and is then peeled to avoid transmitting the odour of its wood to the tobacco leaves. The knots must also be removed from it so that it is smooth and cannot damage the delicate leaves.

Now let's return to the tobacco barn. After drying come the loosening *(zafado)* or tying *(amarre)* — both terms, though contradictory, which serve to designate the same operation. The future quality of the Havana cigar depends heavily on this operation, and it is performed primarily with plants cultivated under cheesecloth or the so-called *sol ensartado*. To this point the leaves have remainèd on the *cujes* — from 1,000 to 1,500 on each one — and now they are taken down.

This has to be done in the morning, before the sun begins radiating much heat, for otherwise, if the leaf is too dry, it could break when touched by the hand. The *zafador* cuts the thread, freeing the leaves and forms them into bunches, used to form fermentation stacks, which vary according to the type of cut.

Tercios, pacas and *barriles*

37. *Interior of a threaded tobacco barn, in various phases of drying, for curing.*

A *tercio* is the solid square package lined with *yaguas* (woody bases of the palm leaf) in which the tobacco leaves are transported from the grading area, or *escogida,* to the stripping site or to the factories or abroad, as in the case of crude tobacco. In this last case, the *tercio* is lined with *arpillera* or burlap. Concerning the job of packing, Ricardo A. Casado tells us:

The enterciadores *(packers) prepare the case by placing two* yaguas *as a base: these* yuguas *form the bottom and top of the* tercio, *with two more on the sides. Then the bundles of leaves are placed carefully (always 80 in a* tercio *of wrappers) and the case closed, after placing the* yagua *on top, properly cut and creased. There the package is triply tied with a sort of cord from the* majagua *or corkwood tree, hence it is also known by the name of that tree.*

It is surprising how much traditional culture and acquired skill there is in each of the tasks needed to produce a Havana cigar. The *yagüero* must strip the *yaguas* from the royal palm to protect the tobacco leaves in their large cases and also in the *tercios* in which it will travel. This peasant knows, among other things, that the *tercio* not only protects the tobacco but also helps keep it fresh and smooth. When it is too humid, the *yagua* is absorbent; when it is too dry, the *yagua* offers some of its own moisture. This is why *yagua* is called the tobacco's thermometer.

The *yaguas* are gathered at the base of the palms, which shed thirteen each year. They must be collected in the early morning, because the humidity keeps them from splitting when handled. The *yagüeros* generally transport them in primitive ox-drawn carts to the processing center. There the *yaguas* are flattened on the floor and then spread to air out.

When dry, they are placed in groups of 200-300, moulded in a press and classified. The packets, tied with twine or the fibers of the bark itself, contain two dozen *yaguas* each.

Then they are transported to the grading barns, where they will serve to pack the tobacco in.

This precious natural resource, so profoundly associated with the quality of the tobacco, had been exported until recently, causing protests from some Cuban tobacco-grower associations from the beginning of this century. On 15 April 1900, for example, the magazine *El Tabaco* expressed its opinion, enabling us to appreciate the enormous quantity of palm bark needed to handle tobacco:

When any country suffers a shortage of an article of domestic consumption, to the extent that its export can cause damaging shortages, as a means of preservation, the exportation of this article is prohibited or, if not totally prohibited, made subject to prohibitive duties. This occurred this year with yaguas *and the extraordinary thing is that the Segretary knew about it. The provinces of Pinar del Río, Havana and Santa Clara, where our tobacco is produced, will nor have sufficient* yagua *this year to pack their tobacco, even purchasing it and paying a good price, from Matanzas and Puerto Principe, where it is produced.*

The three provinces indicated were producing at that time 600,000 *tercios* of tobacco, requiring 3 million *yaguas.*

Barreling is a resting stage that takes place in the stripping barn. The tobacco is aged in *barriles* (barrels) of cedar in fermentation rooms, like wine in cellars.

Each group of 250 tobacco leaves already pressed, stripped, stacked and checked, is placed in a barrel, with a vent-hole in the centre and other holes to allow air to penetrate to the fragrant leaves. They are kept there for around 60 days, according to the texture seclected: *volado, seco, ligero* or *medio tiempo.* When the time comes, the *parrilleros* remove the leaves from the barrels and arrange them in piles, where they will undergo a drying process. They are

37

In the *escogida*

then returned to the barrels and from there go to the End Product Department. Lastly, they are packed in a press.

The *paca* or bale is another way of storing the leaves. While in the *tercio* the tobacco is packed in crude form, in the bales it is stored in stripped or processed form.

The baler places a jute cloth on the surface of a press and then a *yagua;* the tobacco is arranged on top of this and covered with *yaguas* and burlap of jute. The entire bundle is squeezed in the press, reducing the volume of the packed leaves; afterwards more *yaguas* are placed on the sides, double to give the bale form. Lastly, the *paca* is sewn with string or cotton thread.

From the tobacco barn, the leaves are carried to the *escogida* or grading shop, which may be located in the country or in town.

Here the leaves must undergo the following process: preselection, *zafado* (loosening), *moja* (dampening), *oreo* (airing), *reposo* (resting), *selección* (selection), *rezagado* (grading), *picadero* (sorting), *engavillado* (bunching), *manojeo* (bundling), *enterceo* (packing), *fumigación* (fumigation) and *almacenaje* (warehousing), according to the use assigned to the harvested leaf: wrapper, binder or filler. In the *escogidas* the tobacco used for binder and filler is *sol ensartado* from San Juan y Martínez and San Luis.

In the *escogida,* the bunches are grouped according to cut, to avoid mixing.

Then comes the *zafado,* which involves shaking the leaves to separate them before dampening and airing. Then they go to the opening room. The opener selects the leaves that go to form the various classes of wrapper, which go directly to the *rezagado.*

In the *rezagado,* the wrapper leaves, depending on the type of tobacco, are separated by *tiempos, subtiempos* and classes. *Tiempo* means the texture of the tobacco, divided into *ligero* (light), *seco* (dry), *viso* (glossy), *tiempo medio* (average texture) and *amarillo* (yellow). The *subtiempos* are the subdivisions: *ligero viso, ligero seco, ligero viso seco,* etc. The classes may number 40 or 50, depending on the crop of the year and the desired industrial objectives. Cuba has the best classification system in the world for its leaves. They are determined according to the texture, size and grade of flaw and are called, for example, *rezagos once viso seco* (grade 11 glossy dry), *doce viso seco* (12 glossy dry), *trece viso seco* (13 glossy dry), and so forth. For each seven graders there is a checker, who is an experienced worker.

After these operations come the phase called *picadero,* in which the leaves are

38

39. Burro *of black tobacco, in the fermentation process.*

39

40. Preparation of packs (tercios), *formed of bunches of tobacco enclosed in* yaguas.

40

grouped by class. The next day is reserved for the *engavillado*.

A *gavilla* of wrapper leaves is composed of 40 or 50 leaves tied together with a ribbon by their butts.

The bunched leaves, separated by class, are passed in a basket to the *manojeador*. He takes two bunches in each hand and binds them by their butt ends, encircling them with a ribbon. Then he flattens out the leaves, presses them and wraps another ribbon around them till he reaches the end of the bundle, where he finishes off with a knot. This job is true folk art.

Each *escogidas* contains a fermentation center, where the dark leaves are placed on *burros* (saw-horses).

The fermentation technician is the person who supervises and directs the *emburradores* and keeps track of the days the tobacco is on the saw-horses and the quantity of leaves stored there. The fermentation process takes one to three months, depending on the class of tobacco. His task is not an easy one, because he must monitor the temperature on the saw-horses accurately and know what temperature is required for each class to achieve proper fermentation.

The *despalillo* (stripping shop), along with cigar-making, is the heart of the process for creating a Havana cigar.

Part of the *tercios* containing leaves selected as wrappers go directly to the factories; others are transported to the *despalillos*, shops located in various cities, such as Havana, Pinar del Río and Consolación del Sur.

The *sol ensartado de vega fina* tobacco of San Juan y Martínez and San Luis is sent to them.

In the *despalillos* the tobacco leaves are sorted by size, and the broken leaves set aside for use as filler. The separated leaves must be stacked in an orderly fashion, so the bunch is even; then they are placed on a plank and flattened with a press.

The *despalillo* or stripping process consists of removing half the midribs (central veins) of the leaves set aside for filler, a fourth of those designated for binders, and all the midribs removed from the leaves selected as wrappers, forming them into two strips. The cutting is done with a sort of metallic claw, then the midrib is pulled out delicately to avoid breaking the leaf.

41. Selection and grading of the leaves, by size, colour and texture (escogida).

41

How the Havana cigar is born

The *tercios* sent to the factory are opened by *zafadores*. They take the bundles out and proceed to shake the leaves loose from each other: during their processing they have lost much of their moisture and have become brittle. For this reason, they must be dampened, an operation *(moja)* designed to replenish their moisture and facilitate handling. The *mojador* dips the bunches into a tank of water and sprays them with an atomizer. Then the *sacudidor,* using a rhythmic hand movement, without flexing his arm to avoid breaking the leaves, shakes them to expel the water drops remaining on them.

The *moja* process ends in the *orear* (airing) room, where the bunches are hung for around five hours in an environment with 95% humidity.

After the airing, the wrapper leaves go to the stripping shop and then to grading.

The grader expertly classifies barreled wrapper leaves by size and colour, placing them in large wooden boxes; he then places a bunch of leaves on his thigh and, after wetting his hands in a bucket of water, he rubs, stretches and flattens each one, examining it on both sides. He then places the bunch on his thigh again, lines up the leaves and, lastly, places it on the rim of a barrel.

The grader must classify into 18 or 20 classes the tobacco leaves chosen as the precious wrappers which enclose the Havana cigar.

Later, the wrapper counter gathers bunches of 25 leafs, also called *gavillas,* used to manufacture the various *vitolas,* the standard cigar shapes and sizes.

We enter the cigarmakers' room and are compelled to recall the words of Martí: "...there I saw (...) who was reading to the workers, of homeland and moderation, during the work schedule, with a voice neither adulating nor harsh, and he closed the unneeded book and spoke on his own, of the silent majesty of his obscure life, with oratory that was both appeal and judgement, and patriotism heated white-hot (...)".

A preserved tradition of exceptional cultural importance is "reading in the cigar factories". Rivero Muñiz, in an article so entitled, explains its genesis:

The first factory where this was established was "El Figaro", owned by Don José Castillo y Suárez, situated on the corner of Sitios and Angeles (Havana); with the agreement of the 300 cigarmakers who worked in this factory, it was decided that one of them would act as lector *(reader), and that each worker would contribute a corresponding quota to repay the wage that the* lector *failed to earn during the period he was employed in reading, and this was inaugurated on 21 December 1986.*

The culminating task in tobacco processing is that of the cigarmaker. On his rolling table or bench he places a half-leaf of binder. Then he takes between his hands the leaves called *seco* and *volado,* puts the so-called *ligero* in the middle, and wraps them in the binder.

All that remains is covering the cigar: the cigarmaker smooths out the *capa* or wrapper, cuts the edges of the leaf with a semi-circular blade called javetta, utilizing only the centre of the leaf to avoid having veins showing on the outside, and proceeds to wrap the tobacco. He moistens his fingers with just a trace of gum and sticks the edges of the leaf.

The cigarmaker then takes the cigar, now almost finished, and delicately rolls it between his hands to smooth its surface. He passes the flat of the blade to produce a perfect end, but he still must make the *vuelo,* an operation which consists of applying the tip that goes in the smoker's mouth. After attaching the *perilla* or tip with a spot of tragacanth gum, of plant origin, the cigarmaker places the Havana in a small horizontal guillotine and cuts the cigar to the desired length on the end opposite the tip. In a wooden block, he checks that the Havana cigar has the precise dimensions of its *vitola.*

In reality, there are more than 60 *vitolas,* differing in length, diameter and shape. The best known are *Corona, Coronas Grandes, Gran Corona, Dalia, Mareva, Petit Corona, Londres, Prominente, Robusto, Francisco, Placeras, Entreactos, Carolina, Franciscanos, Panetelas Largas, Nacionales, Hermoso Cuatro, Campana, Pirámide, Cervantes, Perla, Delicado, Delicado Extra, Julieta, Carlota, Laguito Number One, Two, Three...* When these types are destined for export, they receive other names, such as: *Churcill de Luxe, Lancero, Panetela, Montecristo Especial, Montecristo Number One, Two, Three, Four, Five,* etc.; *Davidoff 2000, 3000, 4000, Chateau Margaux, Iquen...* and so on, up to a total of 1,000 names known worldwide.

A good cigarmaker can produce more than a hundred elegant Havanas cigar in one day. Once the proper shape and size have been verified, the cigars are tied with a soft ribbon in packets of 50, called a *media rueda* (half-wheel), and go into the vacuum fumigation chamber, where they are immunized against pests.

They are then held in a special case or cabinet *(escaparate)* for three weeks, until they have lost their excess humidity. Appropriately called the great treasure chest of the Havana cigars, the cabinet is under the care of a highly qualified technician who painstakingly attends to the product inside. To give an idea of the complexity of this job, let's say that a four-section cabinet holds around 18,000 cigars.

The person in charge of the cabinet sends the cigars in a wooden container to the Department of Selecting and Packing, also popularly known as *escogida;* where they are graded by colour and boxed. In this operation, new specialists gather the Havana cigars and grade them according to appearence: ochres, terracottas, sienas or browns. A specialist knows, by experience, that no two cigars are the same colour and that a *vitola* may have up to 65 different shades, a full range that the selector must know perfectly. For his task, the selector must take into account first the primary colour and then the secondary shade, an operation called *planteo de la mesa,* by which he compares the cigar he has taken as a model with the others lying on the table. After around a thousand cigars are processed, grouped in horizontal rows, on which up to ten layers of fragrant Havana cigars are placed, the former constitute the classes or hues and the latter the shades of them.

Over the many years, a special nomenclature has been created for each of the cigar hues: *sangre de toro, encendido, colorado encendido, colorado, colorado pajizo, pajizo* and *verde* or *clarisimo;* these are then divided into shades.

When the selector has grouped the cigars by hue and tone, they go to the packer, who matches them even more to present them in chromatic harmony.

Before him on his worktable, the packer places the cedar boxes he must fill meticulously. The darkest cigar is positioned on the left and the lightest on the right. The cigarmaking art requires an additional process, however, for better product presentation: stripping. No unsightly veins must be allowed to show in the wrapper, and the packer will be on the watch for them.

A band identifies each brand and gives rise to such a notable interest as *vitolfilia.* It is said that bands were originally used to protect the fingers of ladies who smoked the delicious Havana cigars long ago.

And as Enrique Hernández Miyares (1859-1914) tells us in his poem *"De sobremesa"* ("After Dinner"):

The cedar box,
With myriad images bedecked,
Half-opened to offer
Its hundred fine fragrant cigars.

42. Groups of packed tercios.

42

43. Zafado *(loosening) of wrapper leaf for moistening, in the factory.*

43

44. Moja *and* oreo *(moistening and airing).*

44

Embellishing the cigar

The first cigars were sold during the period of colonisation in bundles covered with *yagua* or pig bladders, with a capsule of vanilla to make the product more fragrant. Later, rustic cedar chests holding 10,000 cigars were used.

Not until 1850 was luxury packing used. It was apparently banker H. Upmann who had the idea, in 1830, of sending cigars to London, from Havana, in ornamental sealed cedar boxes.

Thus the art of decorative boxmaking was created by an artist named Ramón Allones. Lithography came along to culminate the beauty of the containers, on which a crystalline gloss was obtained by varnishing *a muñeca,* a finish the expert hand of the varnisher obtained by applying various coats of laquer with a *muñeca,* a small wad of cloth soaked in alcohol.

One of the last jobs in the long processing of the Havana cigar is that of boxmaking. More than thirty types of luxury boxes are made. The most elegant is called *Presidencial,* with the official coat-of-arms of the Republica of Cuba, which competes in beauty with another called *Cinco Bocas* (five mouths), because when opened it presents five compartments with a cigar in each. The box called *Humidor,* made of the trunk of cedar, retains the humidity necessary for a good Havana cigar. In addition to these boxes, there are others called *boite nature, semi boite nature con broche* and *corredera* with no decoration or lithography; the cedar bears the trademark and commercial name, imprinted with a steel die.

The typical cedar box in which Havana cigars circle the globe is bedecked inside and out with attractive lithographed labels; then follow the steps known as *terminado, clavado* and *revisado.* The *larguero,* leaf that covers the bottom, and the cover, on the outside, are completed with the decorative border on opening the cover. This operation is called *fileteado.*

White papers called *cabaceros* are glued on the interior sides of the box, and on the upper flap of the *larguero* (the *bufetón*) that covers the cigars. Lastly, the inspector's mark and, on the outside, the seal of quality are added: *"Tabacos habanos genuinos. Vea el sello de garantía del Governo de Cuba en el exterior de este envase"* (Genuine Havana cigars. See the seal of guarantee of the Cuban Government on the outside of this box).

Following the decorating operations, and after drying for 24 hours, the boxes go to the colour selection department mentioned above for filling; after banding, they proceed to the Checking Department and then the process of *clavado* will accomodate the boxes. In the last step, certain quantities of boxes, depending on the *vitolas,* are packed into special cartons.

Good Havana cigars, however, require further care: they are sent to the fumigation and refrigeration facilities where they are stored until their departure overseas.

45. Storing raw material, in barrels.

45

46. Preparation of raw material.

46

Poets and writers celebrate tobacco

Many authors of prose and verse have celebrated the excellent qualities of their companion, smoking, a rare architect that has inspired universal masterpieces of art. In his comedy *Every Man in His Humour*, written in 1598, Ben Johnson tells us:
I have been in the Indies, where this herb grows, and there I and a dozen gentlemen friends of mine tasted no nourishment for twenty-one weeks, except the smoke of this plant. So it must be a divine plant. I can assure you that it heals the rheum, humours and a thousand sorts of maladies. For this reason, I affirm and shall continue to affirm, before any prince of Europe, that tobacco is the most precious plant the earth has ever produced for the use of man.
Lope de Vega (1562-1635), in his play *La mayor desgracia de Carlos V*, has one of his characters say: "Take a little tobacco, your anger will pass".
Charles Perrault (1626-1703), master of children's literature, well known for his stories *Little Red Riding Hood, Cinderella* and others, wrote a poem entitled "Elegy on smoking tobacco":
Tobacco, foe of sadness
Plant that Bacchus sowed,
Social friend of wine,
That animates the feast,
That serves as antidote
To ills, that helps us reason,
That changes worries into delights,
That balm for wounded hearts
It is counted among the vices,
Despite its rare virtues.
Italian humanist Girolan Baruffaldi (1675-1755), in a poem dedicated to tobacco, confesses that in his hours of melancholy "in need of consolation, the frequent use of tobacco afforded him some relief from his cares".
French poet Auguste Barthélmy (1796-1867) composed a *Manual on the Art of Smoking* composed of 5,000 alexandrine verses. We would excerpt the following:

For the man who is not a hapless layman, 'neath the firmament nothing surpasses the Havana cigar.
The sun that browned it swells with pride.
The excellent qualities of the Havana cigar are echoed in the writings of England's Sir Charles Murray. In his book *Visit to Cuba in 1836* he tells us of the English affection for our fragrant leaf. On cigars he states:
...some of the best I have smoked in my life were some cigars given me by an English neighbour here in Havana, cigars which they had sent to Liverpool and which were returned because of their dark colour and ugly appearance. The double trip across the Atlantic cured them sufficiently so that they were the most delicious cigars that even a meditative philosopher could have dreamed.
Lord Byron (1788-1824) ended his poem "Sublime Tobacco" with the following verse: "Give me a cigar".
Thomas Carlyle (1795-1881), conversing one night with Ralph Waldo Emerson (1803-1882), said: "Tobacco is a fine thing, as it permits men to sit together in silence with naught an anxiety. When one has said what he had to say, he can sit back and enjoy his smoking. If this practice were introduced to Parliament, there would be, along with a minimum of discourses, the placid and stimulating influence of tobacco smoke".
A hymn to the Havana cigar and its capital was penned by French writer Marmier (1809-1892). In his book *Papers on America, 1852*, he tells us:
...such indolent pleasure in watching the floating bluish cloud and whitening ash of a good cigar that from the banks of the Seine to those of the Neva, from the coasts of Spain to the plains of North America, the pensive poet, the weary mariner on his watch, the lion of the West End or the Italian boulevards turn their eyes to Havana as a faithful Moslem to Messa.
In the words of novelist George Sand (1804-1876): "Cigars calm pain and people

loneliness with a thousand gracious images".
For Victor Hugo (1802-1885), tobacco "is the plant that converts thoughts into dreams".
Another giant of French literature, Emile Zola (1840-1902), in his work *Rougon-Macquart* states: "I know many great writers who smoke and are quite healthy. If genius is a neurosis, why treat it?".

Rudyard Kipling (1865-1936), bard of Britain's imperial glories of the Victorian age, also alluded to tobacco with great passion. In his poem "The Betrothed", he speaks of choosing between Maggie (love) and tobacco:

But Maggie wrote me telling me to chose
and I know not what to do with my ring
I must chose between love that weeps
and Nicotine, enchanting dame (...)
I know not. May a Havana cigar come to
clear my head (...)
Let's see, a good Havana cigar from its
fragrant box because I wish not Maggie for
my wife.

Thomas Mann (1875-1955), in his famous novel *The Magic Mountain,* has his character Hans Castort say:

I fail to understand how one can live without smoking. It means, undoubtedly, depriving oneself of the best part of existence and, in any case, a very considerable pleasure. When I awake in the morning, I am already happy at the thought that I will be able to smoke during the day; and I have the same thoughts when I eat. Yes, I could say, in a certain way, that I eat so I can smoke afterwards, and I don't think I'm exaggerating much. A day without tobacco would be the height of boredom for me, it would be an absolutely empty, meaningless day.

Belgian novelist and stage actor Maurice Des Ombiaux, in his *Small Treatise on the Havana Cigar* written in 1913, states that "the Havana cigar has never been celebrated as it deserves".

This brief poetic anthology on tobacco would not be complete without Federico García Lorca (1898-1936). In his "Sound of Negroes in Cuba", he evokes the recollection left in his heart by the lovely lithographs he admired as a child on boxes of Havana cigar brands *Fonseca* and *Romeo y Julietta:*

When the full moon comes,
I'll go to Santiago de Cuba,
I'll go to Santiago
in a stage coach.
I'll go to Santiago.
With the blond head of Fonseca.
I'll go to Santiago.
And in the rose-garden of Romeo y Julietta.
I'll go to Santiago.
Sea of paper and shining coins.
I'll go to Santiago.
Oh Cuba! Oh rhythm of dry seeds!
I'll go to Santiago.
Sharp-log harp, alligator, the best tobacco!
I'll go to Santiago.

Herodotos said that Egypt was a gift of the Nile; 3,000 years later poet Narciso Foxá (1822-1863) celebrated tobacco as a "Special gift to Cuba granted".

47. Despalillo *(stripping) of wrapper leaf.*

47

48. Rezagado *(grading) of wrapper leaf.*

48

49. Cigar-maker.

49

Tobacco in plastic art

The pioneer of plastic art on the theme of tobacco was Flemish painter Adriaen Brouwer (1606-1638). His painting "The Smokers", hanging in the Metropolitan Museum of New York, shows a country tavern with soldiers and civilians enjoying beer and tobacco. Other paintings by Brouwer are based on the same motif.

The tradition of Flemish painting based on smoking was carried on by Theodore Rombouts (1597-1637) of Antwerp. His painting "A Smoker", in the Museum of Gant, shows a happy, satisfied man exhaling fragrant smoke.

From the Dutch school we have "Smoking in Society", an oil from the early 17th century by Willem Buytewech (c. 1585-c. 1626), which is exhibited in the Brevius Museum of The Hague.

Jan Steen (1625-1679), in his notable self-portrait, seems to be initiating his son Thaddeus to the ritual of pipe-smoking.

In 1647 Dutch painter Jan van de Velde (1620-1662) completed his "Still Life with Smoking Utensils", with a pipe in the center.

"Singing Smokers" is an ink drawing by Cornelius Dusert (1660-1704).

Throughout the 18th century, Dutch canvases continued portraying Flemish smokers. And in the 19th century, the self-portrait of Vincent van Gogh (1853-1890), precursor of Impressionism, shows him with a pipe in his mouth.

Prominent in France was Gustave Coubert (1819-1877), who entitled his self-portrait in oils "The Pipe Smoker"; Toulose-Lautrec (1864-1901) painted a British soldier with his pipe; Claude Monet (1840-1926) was shown on canvas by Pierre Auguste Renoir (1841-1919), both smoking pipes.

Renoir returned to the theme of smokers in his "After Dinner" where a person, in an Impressionist snapshot, is lighting his cigarette.

Eugène Delacroix (1789-1863), Romantic painter of the Napoleonic period, painted his notable work "Turk Smoking a Pipe".

"The Morning Pipe", a pencil drawing by French painter Honoré Daumier (1808-1879), is rather the caricature of an old man reveling in the smoke blown from his mouth.

The pipe continued to dominate the scenes of smokers with Paul Cézanne (1853-1906), a precursor of Cubism.

Pablo Picasso (1881-1973), the most famous painter of this century, painted "The Smoker" in 1914, with the Cubist style and the collage technique, where he combines fragments of paintings with painted areas. "The Student" and "Newspapers, Vases and Cigarette Packs" are other canvases associated with smoking.

Though the pipe prevailed in European art from Buytewech, it was the Spanish and Cuban masters who put the cigar on their canvases. Basque painter Victor Patricio Landaluze (1828-1889) painted a rich collection of Creole prints in Cuba; one of this works, "The Healer", shows an old woman smoking a cigar as she selects the herbs for preparaing her remedies; in "The Apprentice" he regales us with a young man being initiated to the cigarmaking trade.

Cuban Eduardo Abela (1891-1964), in his oil "The Guajiros", portrays a scene where, among cockfighters and their birds, a horse and a stool, we see a peasant enjoying his cigar.

Armando Menocal (1863-1942), his brush filled with Cubanism, shows a group of beautiful Creoles, white and mulata, working seated: "The Tobacco Strippers".

50. *Gallery of a cigar factory ("reader" in the forefront).*

51. *Quality control.*

50

51

Tobacco in Cuban poetry

To writers José Rivero Muñiz and Andrés de Piedra Bueno we owe the delightful volume *Small Anthology of Tobacco* (1946), a collection of inumerable poems dedicated to the theme of tobacco. It could not be otherwise, because the tobacco-grower and the Havana cigar are a part of Cuba's lyrical soul.

There in the fertile stretch
of riverbank
We watch the tedious grower
transporting the seed of
that grand Havana tobacco.

Thus penned Francisco Poveda y Armenteros (1796-1881).

In his verses "Hatuey y Guarina", Juan Cristóbal Nápoles Fajardo, *El Cucalambé*, 1829-1862, left this scene imprinted on the soul of everything Cuban:

With a fire-beetle in his hand
and a large cigar in his mouth
an Indian from his rock
surveys the Cuban sky.

Gabriel de la Concepción Valdés, *Plácido*, (1809-1844), inspired poet of Matanzas, made his pen sing in "The Pirate's Departure" and describes this scene:

From the stern of a brigantine,
wrapped in his black cape,
smoking pure tobacco
in a silver pipe,
beneath the starting eyes
of a hundred robust men,
stood the greatest chief
that the pirates ever had.

The verses of José Jacinto Milanés (1814-1863) reach the level of

The fragrant leaf
Whose mellow smoke
Quickly relieves man
Of his glowering ennui.

Manuel Gonzáles del Valle (1802-1884), with his Cuba-filled liricism, wrote "Song to Tobacco":

...You return to my lips, o tasty tobacco,
Beloved gift of may homeland,

How often exhausted by sorrow
I've drawn comfort from your influence!
How often in hours
Of love's sweet delirium
In gentle desires,
To your smoke, your fragrant smoke,
My sighs, my moans I've joined!

This young Guarjira girl receives a love philtre in the verses of Ignacio Valdés Machuca (1800-1850):

Ah! give me a cigar, Antonio,
One from the vega,
Next to the river
That waters our farm.
I took it gladly,
Asked him for the candle,
And he with his own mouth
Lit it and passed it to me:
I smoked it and ever since
I know not what
my wretched heart desires,
It throbs so strongly
that it seems determined
to burst from my breast...

Domingo del Monte (1804-1853) was also enamoured with the excellence of our cigars. In *"El Veguero"* he lauds the labors of the tobacco-grower:

At peace cultivating
My beloved fields
On the banks of mighty Cuyaguateje,
My hours flow by
Like the waves of my river
on its course.
And harsh discord
Disturbs not my rest
Nor the cendrada plata
My slumber,
Nor have I ever envied my neighbour;
Beholding my beloved leaf
My weary years are quickly gladdened.

An inseparable companion of a good Havana cigar is the delicious coffee which our land also produces in unquestioned quality. In graceful verses, Miguel Teurbe Tolón (1820-1858) says:

52. Escaparate *or storage case.*

52

53. Finished cigars placed in their storage case.

Between sips, what pure aroma
Rises from a steaming cup of coffee,
Between puffs on a delicious Havana:
The two complement each other,
And both our characters
Sit in savory dialogue
Discussing questions
Of field and farming.
Ricardo del Monte (1828-1909), in his "Ode to Cuban Tobacco", unfurls his imagination:
I am seized by enthusiasm. Immediately
I climb to seventh heaven;
I drean my fantasy. The seed
Grows and expands until it covers the Antille;
And my eyes linger on
Boxes and tercios, *mounds of* manojos,
To fill ships, flood markets;
All races smoking,
United and blissful,
And "smoking", shrouded in fragrant clouds
Of blue vapor that flowing arouses
The whole world, blessing Cuba.
The adventurous imprint of pirates, corsairs and buccaneers is reflected in the lyrics of Bruno Valdés Miranda. In his "Grains of Sand", written in 1894, he revives the bandit Pepe el Mallorquín, who kept his den on the Isla de Pinos:
I still have my cutlass,
My old musket,
Two ounces of powder
I've carefully guarded...
A plug of tobacco,
Passionate tobacco,
Stolen from the British
With fire and blood...
Casimiro Delmonte Portillo (1838-1887) in his "Ode to America" exhalts ... aromatic tobacco:
Universal envy of the globe around
And pride of my homeland alone.
Emilio Ballagas (1908-1954), in "Cuba, Poetry", raises a black chant to the splendid nature of his island and says:
The palpitating, undulating music shakes me like the majá,

Quivering and voluptuous as the surging of your shores.
This fragrance of fresh tobacco causes my eyes to close,
And my blood is excited within me like the red handkerchief of the rumba.
La Abuela (Grandmother), book where I have transcribed the testimony of ancestor Julia de la Osa, reports that in the dancehalls of the last century the young girls adorned their bodices with fragrant tobacco leaves: "The girls of that time, when they went dancing, wore tobacco leaves, which they twisted in the middle to form four small leaves, called *palomitas,* and when they had danced once or twice, they drew them from their bodices to offer to their companions, who took a bite to chew, and they, too, chewed at the dances".
Famed Eduardo Abela (1891-1964), creator of the unforgettable character *El Bobo,* points out in his article "My Reasoning as a Tobacco Smoker": "Finally I can affirm that tobacco, more than a friend who has consoled me in the most adverse moments, is linked to my very thinking and is for me the spring where I can savour the euphoria of living".

54

55. Packaging of cigars. (FOTO SYGMA)

55

56. Banding.

Tobacco and the Cuban nation

Tobacco has always epitomized Cuba. The expression "Cuban ebolition", used in British literature from 1599, identified the fashion of smoking.

Later, it was called Havana and cigar, and ever since the universal seal of elegance unrivaled the world over.

It never ceases to amaze that the word "Cuban" was used in relation to tobacco before it was used to refer to our people. At the same time, the Latin word *cubensis* was used in ecclesiastical charges. In 1795 the genial Creole Francisco de Arango y Parreño used the word *cuban,* though only to designate the whites born here. History had to wait until 1853 before it was applied to the people as a whole, merit that went to black poet and slave Juan Antonio Frías, in his poem "Under the Cuban Sun".

Frías was executed by firing squad in the '70s for his love of national independence. One of the first historical mentions of tobacco in Cuba appeared in the acts of the Havana municipal council of 1557. It speaks of the punishment imposed on female slaves that frequented taverns where tobacco was sold. On 14 May of that year, the Havana authorities agreed to punish female violators with 50 lashes and impose a fine of two pesos on slave-holders who allowed it.

On 20 October 1614, Spanish monarch Philip III issued the Royal Letter that authorized the resumption of tobacco growing but prohibited its trade with foreigners, so that "our Royal Treasury can enjoy the benefit resulting from its commerce"; this product could only be sold in Seville, under penalty of loss of life.

Cuban tobacco history reports that on 15 October 1659, the colonial authorities allowed the planting of tobacco on lands with other crops and imposed a rent on the tobacco growers. Likewise, between the end of that century and the beginning of the next the Governor, Diego de Córdova Lazo de la Vega, was to encourage the development of Havana's growers.

Cuban tobacco had acquired such prestige for its quality that foreign manufacturers mixed leaves from Jamaica, Curaçao, Barbados, Santo Domingo and others with those grown on our island. For this reason, on 17 October 1690, the Spanish crown ordered the Governor of Cuba and the municipal government of Havana as follows: "what you must do is order this city to take all measures to prevent its natives from selling tobacco to foreigners, to mix it, as they do, with that of Virginia and Varinas, without which mixture the foreigners could not sell what they have in those islands".

Thanks to tobacco and its industry, class consciousness began to develop in Cuba, led by the tobacco growers. According to Antonio de Gordón y de Acosta, on 11 April 1717 a regulation was drawn up creating a factory in Havana with branches in Bayamo, Trinidad and Santiago to monopolize all the fragrant product which had previously been manufactured in Seville.

This measure caused the protests of our tobacco growers, and to no avail was the action of the priests who attempted to reassure the Cuban peasants. The outburst came on 21 August 1717 in Jesús del Monte, when the growers marched into Havana crying "Long live Philip V! Down with bad government! Let us be governed by his subaltern!", which compelled the Governor to resign. Only then would the growers return to their lands.

Cuban intellectual José Antonio Portuondo characterized the revolt of the Cuban tobacco growers in their struggle against the monopoly imposed by the Spanish monarchy as "the first great social movement in our country, in the first half of the 18th century, which culminated in 1723 with the hanging of the growers' leaders from the silk-cotton trees of Jesus del Monte, which was then a rural quarter of Havana".

José Rivero Muñiz, in his book *Tobacco: Its History in Cuba,* describes how a group of

57. Dressing up the packaging.

57

58

59. *Sealing of packaging, which identifies and guarantees the product to be original Havana cigar.* (FOTO SYGMA)

59

growers, because of confrontations with the tobacco monopoly, decided to emigrate to the almost unpopulated western regions of Vuelta Abajo, "on which land they began to cultivate from the outset a tobacco of unequaled quality and special aroma, unexceeded by any of those produced in the rest of the world, and thanks to which the Cuban tobacco industry later succeeded in becoming world-famous".

To satisfy the demand of European preferences, Cuba had to be converted into a large plantation for the fragrant leaf. Tobacco fields fluorished in Vuelta Abajo, along the humid shores of the Cuyaguateje, and in the eastern part of the country. Thus developed a series of professions practised by the craftsmen of cigars, cigarettes and snuff. Tobacco powder or snuff, exported largely by the Antilles, also helped tie the young Cuban colony with the economic world of Europe, and ever since, as a Spanish dependency, it was valued primarily as a strategic enclave and not as a producer.

Julio Le Riverend Brusone, in "The Tobacco Mills to 1720", points out that these means of production already existed in Cuba in 1650 and utilized the water power of the La Chorrera river, now called the Almendares. The historian states:

The tobacco mill represented an important step forward in the economic progress of Cuba. Until it appeared, industrial elements were extremely few. It is true to say that as the sugar mill was to the plantation, so the snuff mill was to the tobacco fields. It depended on them as a simple annex incapable of assuming a leading role in the production process; it was necessary, for one thing, because its object was not exactly a conversion of the raw material. At that time the production of powdered tobacco had about the same importance as drying, stacking and bunching the leaves, operations complementary to farming.

The boom in tobacco growing caused a struggle in Cuba between two farming sectors: the *ganaderos* (cattlemen), fuedal landowners, and the *vegueros,* small growers of tobacco and some subsistence crops. The *vegueros* were the ferment of a small agrarian middle class aspiring to abolish the monopolistic system of the king and his colonial support in the Pearl of the Antilles. The interests of the Spanish crown, for its part, caused Philip V to issue a letter patent on 18 December 1740 creating the *Real Compañía de Comercio* (Royal Trading Company), which first monopolized tobacco and then, the following year, all of Cuba's imports and exports.

Such a significant, dramatic event for the Spanish colonial empire in America as the occupation of Havana by the British was one of the fundamental causes for the disappearance of such an odious institution, but with the reinstatement of Spanish dominion on 7 February 1761, the Spanish regime re-established the factory and the controlled sale of tobacco.

From that day on, the tobacco workers of the field and city symbolized the vanguard in the arduous, dramatic journey toward Cuban freedom and played a decisive role in the history of our people.

The tobacco of Vuelta Abajo commanded the highest prices in Europe, so in 1783 the Spanish government installed a new factory in Guane, westernmost city of the country, subordinated to the factory in Havana.

Not until 1818 was the tobacco monopoly abolished, due largely to the activities of Francisco Arango y Parreño and the rebellion of the *vegueros.*

Tobacco, coffee and sugar, three products for the exploitation of humanity, germinated a sort of trinity of good taste in the fertile lands of Cuba and became pillars of the national economy and a fundamental historical factor- and to a great extent they still are.

The production of tobacco, more than any other, demonstrated the tragic truth of the class struggle and the divergencies between

the Spanish metropoli and their Cuban colony: confrontation between the *vegueros* and the *ganaderos* and the economic power of the monarchy, conflict of interests between the rulers and the ruled, struggles of colonial authorities against rising Cuban nationalism, later repeated between the power of the United States and our people. Of singular importance in this historical process was the Cuban-Spanish migration, which began during the 10 Years' War (from 1868), when for important political reasons cigar factories like *Príncipe de Gales* and *La Rosa Española,* with its Creole workers, were set up in the United States, principally in Key West. At the end of the 19th century, 12,000 of the 18,000 workers of Key West were Cubans: they were employed primarily in the tobacco industry and provided firm support to later struggles for independence. Many of them entered the ranks of the Cuban Revolutionary Party, which prepared the War of 1895.

Referring to these self-sacrificing emigrant tobacco-workers, José Martí wrote:

Blessed be these natural men, the only ones with whom great things are accomplished in the world. Only yesterday the craftsmen of Key West granted the result of a day's work to the revolution; and today, when the free schools of San Carlos come to their table, the schools of the House of the People — because Cubans require no instruction in concord and freedom — these general people raise their heads in attention, the Creole heart opens up and the workers' hands open again so the children will not be without teachers: all the children, those of African descent and those of Spanish colour.

Among the signatures printed on the charter of the Cuban Revolutionary Party, founded by emigrants to the United States, we find that of distinguished tobacco worker Carlos Baliño, who in 1925, along with Julio Antonio Mella, founded the Cuban Communist Party.

The order for the revolutionary outbreak of 24 February 1895, beginning of the War of Independence led by Martí, reached Cuba inside a cigar carried to Havana by a brave conspirator. "The content of that cigar inflamed the Revolution of 95", said Gaspar Jorge García Galló in his article "Martí and the Tobacco-workers".

Juan Marinello, in his moving article "The Cuban Tobacco-worker, Militant of Democracy", emphasizes the greater contact our tobacco-workers had with the cultural centers associated with the sugar-industry proletariat and cites the phrase of Martí on those exiled craftsmen in the southern United States who helped create our republic, "invisible and often thankless, with no hope of pay or glory, it is truly pure merit, since we cannot think of it without our hearts filling with love and the homeland with pride". Marinello points out "the self-sacrificing fervour the tobacco-worker has displayed throughout our history" and adds that "we must remember with respect and gratitude the workers of our incomparable leaf who often blazed the trail and showed the way".

When the conflict for independence ceased in 1898, there were 120 important factories in Cuba; four years later, when the U.S. Army left Cuban shores, the capitalists of the United States created the Tobacco Trust, which bought 291 brands of cigars and 85 of cigarettes. Afterwards, the industry survived amid crises and lapses. Suffice it to note that in 1906 258 million cigars were exported, while between 1946 and 1957 the annual average was 44 million.

As they had been in the War of Independence, in the neo-colonial republic the tobacco-workers were an authentic stanchion in the struggle for a freer homeland. And today, together with the workers from other industries, they are building the Socialist Society.

The Havana cigar: from earth to the cosmos

There are still many unanswered questions about the expansion of the aromatic plant, if, for example, it already existed in the Old World before the arrival of Admiral Columbus. In Paris, in 1977, it was announced that during research conducted on the stomach of the mummy of Pharaoh Ramses II, more than 3,000 years old, traces of tobacco leaf were found.

This could indicate some exceptional and highly improbable trade between the ancient cultures of America and Egypt or that tobacco also flourished in the Old World.

In relation to the possible use of tobacco by the Egyptians, some authors such as J.B. Killebrew and H. Myrick maintain the thesis that it was cultivated in the Far East before the arrival of the Spanish in America, although "no convincing proof has been advanced", according to B.C. Akehurst.

The magazine *Le Fumeur* of Brussels reports that in Egyptian tombs of 30 centuries ago, pipes have been found among the offerings, that resemble the modern variety and points out that the Egyptians smoked the leaves of the plantain, rose, jasmin and other fragrant plants. Pharaoh Sesostris is known to have smoked a pipe with lotus leaves more than 3,000 years ago.

It is curious to discover that the Australian Aborigines, before the arrival of the first Europeans, used the leaves of a tobacco species called *Nicotiana suaveolens.*

In the church of Huberville, in the French department of la Manche, we can admire a sculpture of the 11th century, half a millennium before the so-called Discovery of America, that portrays an important person smoking a pipe. The effigy on the tomb of Irish king Thurmond, buried in 1227, shows him in the same pose.

The seeds of tobacco, and of other plants, migrate or travel, sometimes borne by the waters, the wind, birds or by the human hand.

Apparently native to South America, it was diffused by the Indian tribes in North America and the Caribbean; it was transported from Cuba to Europe by Rodrigo de Xerex, as we described earlier. Shortly after the Spanish conquest of Cuba, the sailors who arrived in Havana from all parts of America and Europe purchased tobacco in the taverns of the port. Often, lacking money, the Habaneros bartered tobacco for products from both sides of the Atlantic. Thus began its expansion, and its quality helped it capture the most demanding markets.

Pirates, buccaneers and smugglers, eternal marauders of the Cuban coast, also bartered or stole molasses, hides and tobacco, which from the 16th century was already being grown in the lowlands of Bayamo, Guisa, Trinidad and the hinterland of Havana.

It was more productively introduced to Spain and Portugal by Juan de Toledo. It is a tradition that it was brought home before that by Portuguese Juan Ponce de Léon and that Hernán Cortés sent seeds to Carlos V; the Spanish soldiers of that king helped propagate its use in Germany.

In 1559, Jean Nicot helped it travel from Portugal to France; papal nuncio Cardinal Prospero de Santacroce transported it in the third decade of the 16th century from Portuguese lands to Italy, where it was initially known by the name *erba Santacroce.*

In 1586, pirate Francis Drake, after numerous assualts on Spanish possessions in the New World, took his captured treasure back to England: 240 pieces of artillery and tobacco.

Nonetheless, the introduction of tobacco to England is attributed to Sir Walter Raleigh, of whom it is recounted that a servant doused him with a bucket of water when he saw him smoking, thinking he was on fire. By different paths, the taste for tobacco extended to all the corners of the planet. In 1539 the Spanish Catholic missionaries that

accompanied Francisco Javier diffused the smoking habit among the Japanese, and in 1595 the Portuguese carried the seeds of this solanacea to the Empire of the Rising Sun.

Other mariners of France, England and Holland introduced its cultivation in the rest of the continents, and today it is planted not only in Africa and Asia but also in the temperate climes of Europe, reaching latitudes as high as Sweden and Siberia.

In his delightful article "The Wanderings of Tobacco", Julio Le Riverend Brusone tells us of the marvellous journey of the Havana cigar:

It later set out for the other quadrant: the Havana cigar landed in Venezuela, where it came across the Saxons and Germanics, as it had in the north. In Barinas it was a most cordial encounter.

Mixed with the domestic leaf it was given to Spanish and Dutch merchants; thus it reached the North Sea and the Levantine coasts, still incognito. Not until the 18th century did the final big leap come. It arrived then en masse on the Peninsula, and with it the smugglers, established since then on the banks of the Guadalquivir. It later went further; between France and Spain it was to constitute a country different from both, filled with border wags. Aranda, ambassador at that time, disowned the thousands of Spaniards who lived in Bayonne devoted to the exemplary and edifying illicit traffic of bales and tercios. *Once established in Europe, the Havana cigar took up active participation in continental problems. For the more useless sovereigns of the stale peninsular branch of the Bourbons, a type of Havana cigar was created, the* Regalía de Su Majestad, *the best and of first selection. Thus it was present in Aranjuez, in Bayonne! The holy Alliance enabled Czar Nicholas to smoke the fine* Regalía *cigars. In 1818, amid the conflicts at the Congress of Aix-La-Chapelle, the astute, well-traveled autocrat received 20 cases of Havana cigars, which many of those discussing the fate of*

France must have sampled. And the Duke of Sussex, son of George III, the favourite of the anti-Napoleonic league, also ordered his cases of Regalías, *with which he set himself up as precursor and awakened annunciator.*

From the 16th century, pirates and smugglers helped distribute the fragrant leaf. An event in 1853 indicates the dimensions the traffic against the Spanish royal monopoly had assumed. The brigantine *La Sabina,* with only 11 men aboard, transported 12,000 cigars from Santiago de Cuba to Barcelona, and those sailors declared that they were importing them for their own consumption. In an attempt to avoid such acts, Queen Isabella II of Spain signed a Royal Order dated 16 October 1835, which "provides that it shall not be permitted to embark as rations more tobacco than calculated necessary for consumption by the crew of each vessel".

Germán Arciniegas penned the article "Notes on a Tobacco Leaf" published in Havana in October 1944, which described its expansion from the Old to the New World:

The vice passed from the Indians to the whites. And to the blacks. From the caciques to the lords. The finest lowlands of the Antilles, those of the viceroyships, were reserved for tobacco plantations. Under the transparent air of the tropics, the "broad, thick, mild and velvety" leaves flourished and were cut by the loving hands of the peasants and placed to dry on the ground. Then, under the eaves of the huts they were hung to air, and the eaves, with this brown fringe, quivered under the effect of the warm, mischievous breeze. The aroma of tobacco invaded the roads. The old men, women and children carried it to market like a light load. The shops of the town were perfumed with tobacco. The old women, withered by their years, not by work, sat in the doorway of their hovels and smiled at life sucking on their stogies, balancing the ash, watching the

MADE IN HAVANA, CUBA

MADE IN HAVANA, CUBA

smoke, watching the smoke... As though they were the great lords of England.
And the author of the *Biography of the Caribbean* adds:
All the secrets of America went on being secrets for Europe, except tobacco: it was the only discovery of America. It was the greatest conquest. Hence the reason for the colony and its loss by Spain. The kings wanted to shake hands with the peasants of the tobacco plantations, and a war broke out that split the destinies of the world in two: the American hemisphere was born as a free land and lord of its own responsibility. If the republic became burdensome for the tobacco plantations, revolt broke out again. Freedom came and the fields flourished again, and each cigarette lit is a bud of fire in which new life burns. As though we could turn all the history of four centuries into a pinch of tobacco, pack it into the bowl of a pipe, and watch it float up in spirals of smoke.
The Havana cigar, the genie of poetry and dreams, that travels the pathways of agriculture, industry and commerce, confirming its traveling vocation, has also flown from the earth to the cosmos.
In effect, on 18 September 1980, the Soyuz-38 space vehicle, crewed by Soviet Yuri Romanenko and Cuban Arnaldo Tamayo Méndez, carried the first cigar to extraterrestrial space. The Cuban tobacco industry produced an Havana cigar of the *vitola* traditionally called "Corona", 144 mm long and 16.67 mm in diameter.
In its preparation, the filler selected was leaf from the famous tobacco farms of San Juan y Martínez and San Luis; for the binder, leaves grown in the *finas* plantations of Santa Damiana, of the celebrated Vuelta Abajo area. The silky, delicate wrapper was harvested in the area of Partido, municipality of San Antonio de los Baños, province of Havana.
The band and the lithographed *banda,* specially designed for the First Cuban-

Soviet Joint Space Flight, with the colours blue, white and red, bore in its centre the resplendent white star of the Cuban flag, which will thus, from star to star, reach the farthest galaxies of the boundless universe.

"Bibliography"

ABELA, EDUARDO "Mis razones como fumador de tabacos". Revista *Habano,* Vol. XVII; No. XII, La Habana, diciembre de 1951, p. 30-33.

"ABONOS PARA EL TABACO". Revista *El Tabaco,* La Habana, mayo 25 de 1900, p. 13.

ACADEMIA DE CIENCIAS DE CUBA. INSTITUTO DE SUELOS. *Génesis y clasificación de los suelos de Cuba.* La Habana, 1973. 315 p.

AGUAYO, R.C. *Manual del cultivo del tabaco.* Ponce, Puerto Rico, 1876. 78 p.

AKEHURST, B.C. *El tabaco. Agricultura tropical.* Barcelona, 1973. 682 p.

"AL PRESIDENTE LINCOLN LE GUSTABA EL TABACO". Revista *El Tabaco,* Año XXVII; No. 23. La Habana, 10 de diciembre de 1920, p. 27.

ARCINIEGAS, GERMAN. "Apuntes sobre una hoja de tabaco". Revista *Tabaco,* Año XII, No. 137. La Habana, octubre de 1944, p. 23-28.

—. *América en Europa.* Bogotá, Plaza and Janes, 1980. 303 p.

AVENDAÑO HUBNER, JORGE. "El tabaquismo: problema social". *El Comercio,* Lima, diciembre 5 de 1980.

BACARDI, EMILIO. *Crónicas de Santiago de Cuba.* Santiago de Cuba, 1925, tomo II.

BALMASEDA, FRANCISCO JAVIER. *Tesoro del agricultor cubano. Manuales para el cultivo de las principales plantas propia del clima de la Isla de Cuba.* La Habana, 1890, 1892 y 1896, tomo I, 324 p. tomo II, 438 p., tomo III, 440 p.

BEDRINANA, FRANCISCO C. *Vida y aventura de Rodrigo de Xerez. Historia novelada del descubrimiento del tabaco.* Madrid, 1952. 188 p.

BLANCO FERNANDEZ, ANTONIO. *Manual de Agricultura.* La Habana, 1868. 236 p.

BENDOYRO, RALBERTO. "La cohiba cumple 500 años". Periódico *Juventud Rebelde,* La Habana, diciembre 4 de 1983, p. 6.

BENEFICIO Y MANIPULACION DEL TABACO. La Habana, 1975. 54 p.

BENNETT, H.H. y R.V. ALLISON. *Los suelos de Cuba y algunos nuevos suelos de Cuba.* La Habana, 1966. 375 p.

CARDOSO, ONELIO JORGE. "Una historia en tres tiempos". Revista *Cuba Tabaco,* No. 40. La Habana, 1981, p. 36.

CASADO, RICARDO A. *Nuestro tabaco. El Habano sin igual.* La Habana, 1939. 171 p.

CASAS, FRAY BARTOLOME DE LAS. *Historia de Las Indias.* Madrid, s/f, tomo I, 608 p.

"150 AÑOS DE VIDA Y 140 DE FUMADOR". Revista *Habano,* Vol. IX; No. XII. La Habana, diciembre de 1943, p. 32.

COBO, CRISTOBAL. *Historia del Nuevo Mundo.* Sevilla, Sociedad de Bibliófilos Andaluces, 1890-1895, 4 volúmenes.

COLON, CRISTOBAL. *Diario de navegación.* La Habana. Comisión Nacional Cubana de la UNESCO, 1961, 221 p.

"COMO FUMAN ALGUNOS PERSONAJES". Revista *El Tabaco,* Año XLV; No. 7-8. La Habana, 25 de abril de 1938, p. 4.

COROMINAS, J. y J.A. PASCUAL. *Diccionario crítico etimológico castellano e hispánico.* Madrid, 1980, vol. 3.

CORTI, COUNT. *A History of Smoking.* New York, Harcourt, Brace and Company, 1932. 296 p.

CORTINA, HUMBERTO. *Tabaco, historia y psicología.* La Habana, 1939, 129 p.

CREEFF, DR. J.H. "Ni el tabaco ni el alcohol impiden llegar a los cien años". Revista *Tabaco,* Año III, No. 31. La Habana, diciembre de 1935, p. 14.

CUBAS y GARCIA, MANUEL. *Cultivo del tabaco.* La Habana, 1898. 138 p.

DAVIDOFF, ZINO. *Histoire du Havane.* Tolosa, 1981, 107 p.

"DESDE LOS 500. DE COMO EL VEGUERO CONOCE LOS SECRETOS DEL TABACO". Revista *Cuba Tabaco.* Epoca II, No. 10, La Habana, abril-junio de 1974, p. 44.

"DESDE LOS 500. ZOLA Y EL TABACO". Revista *Cuba Tabaco,* Epoca II, No. 10, abril-junio de 1974, p. 45.

"DESDE LOS 500. LOS MAS DELICIOSOS PUROS". Revista *Cuba Tabaco,* Epoca II, No. 10. La Habana, abril-junio de 1974, p. 45.

DICCIONARIO ENCICLOPEDICO HISPANO-AMERICANO DE LITERATURA, CIENCIAS, ARTES, ETC. Editores Montaner y Semor, Barcelona y W.M. Jackson, Inc., Nueva York. Tomo XIII, 1007 p.

"EL CANCER Y EL FUMAR".. Revista *El Tabaco,* Año XXI; No. 18. La Habana, 25 de septiembre de 1914, p. 43.

"EL FUMAR Y EL ATLETISMO". Revista *El Tabaco,* Año XXXIII; No. 1, La Habana, 10 de enero de 1926, p. 7.

"EL TABACO". Revista *Tabaco,* Año VIII. No. 84, La Habana, mayo de 1940, p. 5-34.

"EL TABACO DE CUBA EN ESPAÑA". Revista *El Tabaco,* La Habana, abril 15 de 1900, p. 25.

"EL TABACO EN LA GUERRA". Revista *El Tabaco,* Año XI, No. 3. La Habana, 10 de febrero de 1904, p. 7.

"EL TABACO Y LOS HOMBRES DE GENIO". *Revista Tabaco,* Año III, No. 30. La Habana, noviembre de 1935, p. 26.

"EL ORIGEN DEL TABACO". Revista *El Tabaco,* Año XXI, No. 21. La Habana, 10 de noviembre de 1914, p. 33.

"EL PRIMER TRATADO SOBRE EL TABACO". *Revista Tabaco,* Año I, No. 9. La Habana, diciembre de 1933, p. 11.

"EL PROFESOR ALBERTO EINSTEIN USA UNA PIPA RECTA Y LARGA QUE LO ACOMPAÑA JUNTO AL LAPIZ QUE SIEMPRE LLEVA EN EL BOLSILLO". *Revista El Tabaco,* Año XXXVIII, No. 1, La Habana, 10 de enero de 1931, p. 17.

EMERSON, ELLEN. *Indian myths.* Londres, 1884.

FEINHALS, JOSEPH. "Del tabaco y sus devotos". *Revista Habano.* Vol. IV, No. 1, La Habana, enero de 1938, p. 38.

FERNANDEZ DE MADRID, DON JOSE. *Memoria sobre el comercio, cultivo y elaboración del tabaco de esta Siempre Fiel Isla de Cuba.* La Habana, 1822. 44 p.

"FUMADORES DE HOY Y FUMADORES DE AYER". *Revista Tabaco,* Año 1, No. 7. La Habana, octubre de 1933, p. 2.

GARCIA GALLO, GASPAR JORGE. *Biografía del Tabaco Habano.* Universidad Central de Las Villas, 1959. 213 p.

—. *Biografía del tabaco.* La Habana, 1961. 293 p.

GORDON Y DE ACOSTA, D. ANTONIO DE. *El tabaco en Cuba. Apuntes para su historia.* La Habana, 1897. 85 p.

GORNES MAC-PHERSON, MARTIN JOSE. *De la Conquista a nuestros días.* Caracas, Editorial Elite, 1933. 437 p.

GUEVARA, ERNESTO CHE. *Obras. 1957-1967.* La Habana, Casa de las Américas, 1970. Colección Nuestra América, tomo I, 630 p.

HAZARD, SAMUEL. *Cuba a pluma y lápiz.* Colección de Libros Cubanos, Vol. VII, VIII y IX. La Habana, 1928.

HUMBOLDT, ALEJANDRO DE. *Ensayo político sobre la Isla de Cuba,* nueva edición con un mapa, traducido al castellano por José López de Bustamante. Paris, Leconte y Lasserre, 1840. 361 p.

IRAIZOZ, ANTONIO. "Los fumadores en la pintura clásica". Revista *Habano,* Vol. XVI; No. XII. La Habana, diciembre de 1950. p. 24-25.

JACOBO I DE INGLATERRA. "Anatema contra el tabaco". Revista *Tabaco,* Año VIII, No. 80. La Habana, enero del 1940, p. 13-40.

JIMENEZ PASTRANA, J. *La rebelión de los vegueros.* Serie Martí. La Habana, Editora del Ministerio de Educación, 1962. 14 p.

—. "La rebelión de los vegueros". La Habana, 1979. 69 p.

JUAN, ADELAIDA DE. *Pintura y grabados coloniales cubanos.* La Habana, 1974, 81 p.

"La ley contra los cigarrillos". Revista *El Tabaco,* Año XXVIII, No. 16. La Habana, 25 de agosto de 1921, p. 17.

"LA PROHIBICION AUMENTA EL CONSUMO DEL TABACO". Revista *El Tabaco,* Año XXVII, No. 1. La Habana, 10 de enero de 1920, p. 35.

LAPLANTE, EDUARDO. *Los ingenios.* La Habana, 1857.

LE RIVEREND, JULIO. "Periplo del tabaco". Revista *Habano,* Vol. VI, No. XII. La Habana, diciembre de 1940, p. 22-23.

"LEYENDA INDIA SOBRE EL TABACO". Revista *El Tabaco,* Año XXVIII, No. 18. La Habana, 25 de septiembre de 1921, p. 27.

"LOS EFECTOS DEL TABACO". Revista *El Tabaco,* Año XLV, No. 1 y 2. La Habana, enero 25 de 1938, p. 38.

"LOS FUMADORES DE HACE 3000 AÑOS". Revista de *El Tabaco,* Año XI, No. 7. La Habana, 10 de abril de 1904, p. 9.

MACKENZIE, COMPTON. *Sublime Tobacco.* London, Chatto and Windus, 1957. 352 p.

MADARIAGA, SALVADOR DE. *Vida del muy magnífico Señor Don Cristóbal Colón.* Buenos Aires, 1944, 657 p.

MARTI, JOSE. "Observaciones sobre el hábito de fumar, cigarrillos de papel". *Obras completas. Tomo 8, Nuestra Amériica. La Habana, 1975,* p. 410.

"MARTI, LOS TABAQUEROS Y LA REVOLUCION DE 1895". Revista El Tabacalero, Año 2, No. 19. La Habana, febrero 1ro. de 1946, p. 2.

MARTIN, JUAN LUIS. "La vieja leyenda del tabaco". Revista *Tabaco,* Año XI, No. 124. La Habana, septiembre de 1943, p. 9.

MAS Y OTZET, FRANCISCO. *El tabaco y la industria tabaquera en Cuba.* La Habana, 1886. 51 p.

"MENSAJE DE SIBELIUS". Revista *Habano,* Vol. XV, No. V, La Habana, mayo de 1949, p. 7.

MILSANIA. "Los oficios. La Liga". Revista *Cuba Tabaco,* Epoca II, No. 43. La Habana, 1982, p. 34.

MILSANIA. "Desde los 500. La Condesa de Merlin y el tabaco". Revista *Cuba Tabaco*. Epoca II, No. 56. La Habana, octubre-diciembre de 1985, p. 35.

MILSANIA. "Desde los 500. Tabaco de contrabando". Revista *Cuba Tabaco*. Epoca II, No. 56. La Habana, octubre-diciembre de 1985, p. 35.

"NAPOLEON BONAPARTE, BENEFACTOR DEL TABACO". Revista *El Tabaco*, Año XIV, No. 1-2. La Habana, enero 25 de 1938, p. 16.

NUÑEZ JIMENEZ, ANTONIO. "Descubrimiento del tabaco". Revista *Habano*, vol. XI, No. XII, La Habana, diciembre 1945.

—. *Geografía de Cuba. Cuarta parte. Geografía Económica*. 4ta. edición, La Habana, 1973, 719 p.

—. *La abuela. Narraciones*. Lima, 1973. 237 p.

ORAMAS, ADA. "De entre mitos y leyendas, todo un personaje: el tabaco". Revista *Cuba Tabaco*, Epoca II, No. 10. La habana, abril-junio de 1974, p. 10-23.

—. "Habla José A. Portuondo. Del tabaco y sus hombres: historia, literatura". revista *Cuba Tabaco*, Epoca II, No. 15. La Habana, julio-septiembre de 1975, p. 5-7.

—. "Los oficios. El ensarte". Revista *Cuba Tabaco*, Epoca II, No. 18. La Habana, octubre-diciembre de 1975, p. 54.

—.. "Los anillos de tabaco. Un arte de siglos reviste el Habano". Revista *Cuba Tabaco*, Epoca II, No. 18, Abril-junio de 1976, p. 4-10.

—. "Los oficios. El planchado de jicotea". Revista *Cuba Tabaco*, Epoca II, No. 18, La Habana, abril-junio de 1976, p. 24.

—. "Los oficios. El revisado de apartadura". Revista *Cuba Tabaco*, Epoca II, No. 19, La Habana, julio-septiembre de 1976, p. 33.

—. "Los oficios. El adorno de cajas". Revista *Cuba Tabaco*, Epoca II, No. 20, La Habana, octubre-diciembre de 1976, p. 24.

—. "Los oficios. El emburrado". Revista *Cuba Tabaco*. Epoca II, No 27. La Habana, julio-diciembre de 1978, p. 41-42.

—. "Los oficios. El rezagado de capa". Revista *Cuba Tabaco*. Epoca II, La Habana, julio-septiembre de 1979, p. 38.

—. "En el mágico universo del indio colombiano". Revista *Cuba Tabaco*. Epoca II, No. 32. La Habana, octubre-diciembre de 1979, p. 42-50.

—, "Los oficios. El empacador". Revista *Cuba Tabaco*, Epoca II. No. 33. La Habana, enero-marzo de 1980, p. 39.

—. "Los oficios. El revisado de deshile". Revista *Cuba Tabaco*, No. 40, La Habana, 1981, p. 30.

—. "Los oficios. El anillado a máquina". Revista *Cuba Tabaco*, Epoca II, No. 42. La Habana, 1982, p. 33.

—. "Los oficios. El responsable de escaparate". Revista *Cuba Tabaco*, Epoca II, No. 44. La Habana, 1983, p. 28.

—. "Los oficios. El tendido del tabaco". Revista *Cuba Tabaco*, Epoca II, No. 47, La Habana, 1983, p. 34.

—. "Los oficios. La revisión del engavillado". Revista *Cuba Tabaco*. Epoca II, No. 48. La Habana, 1983, p. 38.

—. "Los oficios. El deshije". Revista *Cuba Tabaco*, Epoca II, No. 49. La Habana, 1984, p. 50.

—. "Los oficios. El empilonado". Revista *Cuba Tabaco*. Epoca II, No. 51. La Habana, 1984, p. 42.

—. "Los oficios. El resecador de tabaco rubio". Revista *Cuba Tabaco*, Epoca II, No. 50, La Habana, 1984, p. 29.

—. "Los oficios. El pesaje del tabaco". Revista *Cuba Tabaco*. Epoca II, No. 52. La Habana, 1984, p. 18.

ORTIZ, FERNANDO. *Contrapunteo cubano del tabaco y el azúcar*. La Habana, Consejo Nacional de Cultura, 1963. 540 p.

PAULA ARIAS, DON ANTONIO MARIA DE. *El veguero de Vuelta Abajo. Apuntes sobre el cultivo del tabaco o breve reseña de las causas de la depreciación del fruto y del sistema que para aquél se estableció*. Pinar del Río, 1887, 120 p.

PELAEZ, ROSA ELVIRA. "Del viaje en carabelas al viaje por el Cosmos, como símbolo singular de lo cubano, tenemos al Puro Habano". Periódico *Granma*.

PERDOMO, JOSE E. *Léxico tabacalero cubano*. La Habana, 1940, 163 p.

—. "La riqueza tabacalera cubana". Revista *Habano*, Vol. XIX, No. V. La Habana, mayo de 1953, p. 17.

PEREZ DELGADO, NICOLAS. "El desconocido oficio del yagüero". Revista *Cuba Tabaco*, Epoca II, Año II, No. 5, La Habana, enero-marzo de 1973, p. 46-55.

PEREZ PEREZ, ROMAN. *El cultivo del tabaco en Cuba*. La Habana, Ministerio de Agricultura, mayo de 1944. 67 p.

PEZUELA, JACOBO DE LA. *Diccionario geográfico, estadístico, histórico de la Isla de Cuba*. 4 tomos. Madrid, 1863-66.

"PLANTAS FUMABLES, SUS EFECTOS TERIBLES O EXTRAÑOS". Revista *El Tabaco*, Año XI, No. 7. La Habana, 10 de abril de 1904, p. 7.

QUINTELA, CARLOS. "Con los cujeros de la costa". Revista *Cuba Tabaco*, Epoca II, No. 15, La Habana, julio-septiembre de 1975, p. 16-23.

RIVERO MUÑIZ, JOSE. "El tabaco en Rusia". Revista *Tabaco,* Año II, No. 12. La Habana, marzo de 1934, p. 11-20.

—. "La lectura en las tabaquerías". Revista *Tabaco,* Año II, No. 21. La Habana, diciembre de 1934, p. 17-18.

—. "Martí y los hombres del tabaco". Revista *Habano,* Vol. XIX, No. 1. La Habana, enero de 1953, p. 10-11.

—. *Tabaco. Su historia en Cuba.* 2 tomos. La Habana, 1964.

RIVERO MUÑIZ, JOSE y ANDRES DE PIEDRA-BUENO. *Pequeña antología del tabaco.* La Habana, 1946. 135 p.

"RAMSES II MASCABA TABACO". Periódico *La Prensa,* Lima, junio 17 de 1977.

RIJO, SEVERO. "El tabaco en el Amazonas". Revista *Tabaco,* Año IX, No. 96. La Habana, mayo de 1941, p. 31.

ROIG Y MESA, JUAN TOMAS. *Diccionario botánico de nombres vulgares cubanos.* La Habana, 1962. Tomo II, 1142 p.

ROSA, MIGUEL LA. "Los oficios. El enterceo del tabaco". Revista *Cuba Tabaco,* Epoca II, No. 10. La Habana, abril-junio de 1974, p. 56.

—. "Los oficios. El enmantado". Revista *Cuba Tabaco,* Epoca II, No. 15. La Habana, julio-septiembre de 1975, p. 30.

—. "Los oficios. El clasificado y envase". Revista *Cuba Tabaco,* Epoca II, No. 17. La Habana, enero-marzo de 1976, p. 31.

—. "Los oficios. El cobijador". Revista *Cuba Tabaco.* Epoca II, No. 32. La Habana, octubre-diciembre de 1979, p. 33.

—. "De cuando en Vuelta Abajo apareció un tesoro del mundo". Revista *Cuba Tabaco,* Epoca II, No. 46. La Habana, 1983, p. 31.

TOMAS, ANGEL. "La yerba del diablo". Periódico *Juventud Rebelde.*

"UN CANTO AL TABACO". Revista *El Tabaco,* Año XIX, No. 11. La Habana, 10 de junio de 1912, p. 25. (Tomado de la *Concordia,* de Buenos Aires).

"UNA BULA PAPAL CONTRA EL TABACO". Revista *Tabaco,* Año VII, No. 75. La Habana, agosto de 1939, p. 29.

Acknowledgements

The author wishes to express his gratitude to the friends of the Empresa Cubatabaco for their sustained help throughout the preparation of this work.

To Mercedes Sánchez Villoch, for her collaboration during the period of preparation.

To poet Pablo Armando Fernández, Reinaldo Pérez Machado, Luisa Fernández Molina, Eugenio Pérez Ferrer and Angel Graña González for reviewing the original text.

For the parts concerning the cultivation and processing of tobacco, we wish to thank the friends of the Department of Agrotechnics of the National Agricultural Office of Tobacco, the Ministry of Agriculture and the specialists in tobacco processing at the Unión de Empresas del Tabaco.